Praise for
FANNY RULES

"*Fanny Rules: A Mother's Leadership Lessons that Never Grow Old* is a must-read for purpose-driven leaders. Dr. Troy's transformative leadership principles shine through as he relates them to stories of his late mother's wisdom. These lessons give us all a glimpse into the type of powerful leadership legacy that we can leave behind for others to use. Fanny Rules are hands-on lessons that can help leaders navigate their personal and professional lives, and a refreshing breakaway from the traditional business book. A touching tribute to a woman whose clarity, confidence, and self-awareness set an example for us all...this book is simply a joy from start to finish."

—ASHLEY RHODES-COURTER
NY Times Bestselling author of *Three Little Words*

"*Fanny Rules* is an engaging tale of triumph over tribulation, happiness out of heartbreak, and love over loss. Dr. Troy brings meaning to life's often tragic twists—honoring his wonderful mother by passing on her wisdom for generations of leaders to come."

—MARK PETTIT
Bestselling Author, EMMY® Award-winner, & Actor

"In every book you read, you would normally ask yourself what part, what joke or anything at all that stood out. With no exaggeration, *Fanny Rules* is the real deal! It may simply be because of its practical use of life lessons, relatable ⋯⋯⋯⋯ me."

—KONSTANTIN CO
Development Educato⋯ the
Philippines

D1113248

"Dr. Troy can integrate the inspirational teaching of his mother with modern-day leadership needs. I loved reading the book because it's true to life application of the skills we need as a leader. I love the nineth one—'Finding Yourself.' It's a great source of motivation. It helps us focus on the positive drivers of behaviors that add value to people, especially the people we want to influence for the better. The book is a reminder that the people we lead would only value our leadership if they know we care and value them. Dr. Troy, thanks for sharing the wisdom of your mom, Fanny."

—ELENITA V. SAN ROQUE
Chief Executive Officer, Association of Asian Confederation of Credit Unions

"Fanny Rules is inspiring, heartfelt, and filled with wisdom. If you are looking for a great story that teaches you timeless leadership lessons without the mundane lecture feel, *Fanny Rules* is a must read and makes me think about the one word I have always used in reference to leadership, RESPONSIBILITY! Fanny demonstrates for all of us that no matter the circumstance, when you are a leader your responsibility is to the people you lead. Leaders around the world will be endeared to Fanny as well as forever changed by her wisdom, just as I have been."

—KENYA DUNN
Chief Executive Officer PFW Coaching & Consulting

"A touching, fun and beautiful book about leadership and life. Dr. Troy shares stories and lessons that demonstrate what true leadership is really all about."

—MICHAEL ZIPURSKY
Co-Founder, Consulting Success®

"*Fanny Rules: A Mother's Leadership Lessons that Never Grow Old* is a tool and a mentorship playbook that I have taken to heart and used in my day-to-day life. I would recommend it to everyone looking for insight on leadership training and guidance. "The truth is in the 'I am' not in the someday 'I will be,'" and to be a leader you need to believe in yourself and begin the journey today."

—DAVID S. MATEGWA, OGW, DSA, ICUDE
National Chairman, Kenya Police, Sacco

"Dr. Troy's down-to-earth storytelling style, combined with the actionable items at the end of each chapter, have the impact of taking boyhood advice from his mom and transforming it into golden success nuggets that anyone can utilize to build their careers, their business, their brands, and, quite honestly, their relationships."

—CURT MERCADANTE
Bestselling Author of *Five Pillars of the Freedom Lifestyle: How to Escape Your Comfort Zone of Misery*, Principal and Founder, Merc Enterprises

"*Fanny Rules* is a must-read for every business leader. Filled with powerful memories starting from a boy sitting at his mother's deathbed, these stories will make you laugh, cry, and grow. Filled to the brim with parables and principles, Fanny was a leader for the ages. We are lucky her wisdom was passed down through her son in a heartfelt and remarkable way. You won't be able to put this book down."

—WHITNEY MCDUFF
Speaker Brand Strategist, Public Relations, Bestselling Author of *The Lollie Tree*

"Filled with practical wisdom told through compelling and relatable storytelling, Dr. Troy shares profound lessons through a lens of humor. I had a grin on my face from the first line of the book. This is a welcome break from traditional slumber-inducing leadership books. *Fanny Rules* is a must-read for professionals at all levels who are ready to smile while succeeding."

—DOUG FALVEY
Senior Vice President of Operations, Allied Solutions

"Time-honored wisdom never changes. Although the economy, environment, and politics change the basic rules for success stay the same. In *Fanny Rules*, Dr. Troy relates those truths and lays out a path for your success. Success is an elusive concept and is different for every individual. No matter what your goal in life, *Fanny Rules* will give you direction on how to achieve your dream. I highly recommend this book."

—COACH ROY AUSTIN, CPA, CMA, MBA
Rockwell Business Solutions, Founder/Chair Libraries For Kids Int'l, Author of *The Alligator Business Solution–Small Business Competitive Edge*

"I found that once I started reading, I could not put *Fanny Rules* down. Although I did not have the privilege of knowing Fanny, I feel as though I have known her for years through the intimate details and life lessons in this book. As a wife, mother, and leader, this book touched my soul to the point of tears. This book will be part of my treasured collection."

—JENNIFER OLMEDA, VP
Area Sales & Service, South Carolina Federal Credit Union

"*Fanny Rules* is a poignant tale of Dr. Troy's path to leadership. It resonated with me personally because my mom was also called "Fanny," and she had Alzheimer's as well. When I became a Client Manager, my late husband who was a Captain in the Fire Department, always told me, "It's not rocket science." The many words of wisdom will stick with you with their humor and relevance. Moms always know, don't they, with their "supersonic hearing" and eyes behind their head! This read is not only for leaders, but for anyone just wanting to be a better person, not a "donkey," and learn how to catch more bees with honey than vinegar. Dr. Troy's mom, Fanny, was a wise woman. I wish I had the chance to meet her in person"

—MARIE SCOTT
Author, Speaker, & Wellness Coach

"This amazing book filled with practical advice passed down from mother to son is sure to inspire generations to come."

—ADAM TORRES
Co-Founder of Mission Matters Media, International speaker, Author of multiple bestselling books and host of the *Mission Matters* podcast series

"From start to finish, *Fanny Rules* is chock full of stories that capture the heart. The book is relatable and impactful. It not only highlights important lessons for business leaders, it also makes a great guide for parents, highlighting the significant role mothers play in their children's lives and how to raise independent thinkers with integrity."

—STACEY CREW
Author Advocate, Bestselling author of *The Organized Mom* and *Mind Body Kitchen: Transform You & Your Kitchen for Healthier Eating*

"*Fanny Rules* endorses two very basic principles…keep it simple and look for teachable moments everywhere! What a wonderful guide to developing leadership skills. Life lessons creating leadership lessons. If we simply follow Fanny's "rules," life and leadership would be so much easier, and we'd fill a leadership emptiness in today's environment. *Fanny Rules* is interactive. You definitely should give it a try. I've always believed leadership is a contact sport! To be actionable, plans need to be simple and easy to execute. You need to practice, practice, practice to allow your skills to develop naturally. *Fanny Rules* shares teachable moments in every chapter and provides exercises to give you the opportunity to challenge yourself and practice new skills. Fanny also espouses that a little grit doesn't hurt, either. How wonderful that Dr. Troy is so comfortable in his own skin that he's willing to "bare it all" in *Fanny Rules* so we too can take advantage of the life lessons he learned from his mother. A huge thank you."

—LINDA VERBA, EVP
Head of Service Strategy TD Bank, Retired

"*Fanny Rules* is a total home run. Dr. Troy brings his best leadership advice in the form of heartfelt stories that encourage and inspire us all to be a better version of ourselves. As both a business leader and family man, I found these stories charming, relatable, and actionable. This needs to be a staple of every leadership team and discussed at every kitchen and negotiation table. Bravo, Dr. Troy!"

—PAUL RUTTER
Executive Coach, Keynote Speaker, & Author of *You Can't Make This Ship Up*

"In his latest book, *Fanny Rules*, Dr. Troy reflects upon the life of his mother, Fanny, and how her superb example takes the reader through a lifetime of boldly facing and negotiating circumstances and situations. By making the decision to appropriately face such challenges, Fanny demonstrates a perpetual learning process, reminding us that opportunities never present themselves on our terms. Decisions must be made, and consequences are guaranteed, regardless if we decide to act or remain idle. Drawing from the Nine Lessons, Dr. Troy relates how anyone can cut his or her own path of leadership by tailoring the journey for the reader. *Fanny Rules* provides a simplistic process, leading one to ultimately discover the single ingredient needed to reach the highest levels of leadership and success. I highly recommend Dr. Troy's work of transparency, and how he shares the journey of Fanny's difficulty, as the reader will be eager to learn how true leadership and promotion is ultimately grasped...not birthed."

—DR. MIKE GILBERT
Consultant, Founder and Leader, The Well

"Teachable moments shape our daily virtues. Dr. Troy shares these lessons taught by his biggest mentor, his mother, in his newest book, *Fanny Rules*. The simplest lessons are the ones we forget, yet the ones we need most to guide us in making discerning decisions. The book outlines nine lessons that apply from childhood through adulthood. I hope to pass these lessons on to our daughter."

—SARAH EVANS SPRINKLE
Strategic Planning and Fundraising Consultant

"What an amazing, uplifting and refreshing book!! It filled my heart with joy and love. *Fanny Rules: A Mother's Leadership Lessons that Never Grow Old* is a must read to learn or be reminded of the basics of leadership AND living one's life with integrity and a love for others. How I wish I could have met Fanny! Dr. Troy Hall is an eloquent writer who so succinctly describes the Life Lessons his wise mother, lovingly nick-named "Fanny," taught him and instilled in him throughout his childhood. A very simple outlined inspirational guide of traits that we all should live by. These are pertinent to any age and can be reviewed multiple times throughout one's life. An amazing, lighthearted book with many principles to live by."

—DONNA CLERVI
Certified Parkinson's Fitness Specialist, Owner of Rock Steady Boxing, M.E. Boxing & Fitness

"*Fanny Rules: A Mother's Leadership Lessons that Never Grow Old* is the modest title of the new book by Dr. Troy Hall. Modest because the life lessons in this book are like a leprechaun finding the end of a rainbow—they are multitudinous and overflowing. Troy shares numerous lessons he learned from his mother Fanny and applied throughout his life. He has included many of these stories for us to cherish and perhaps recall some of the lessons we too learned growing up. If you need a guidebook of common sense, feel good wisdom, there is no better book."

—HOWARD H. PRAGER
Executive Coach & Author of *Make Someone's Day: What It Can Do For You and Your Company*

"It's not often someone comes along and stops you in your tracks. Dr. Troy Hall is one of those people—he literally stops you in your tracks. Dr. Troy is an inspiration, he is infectious, he makes you want to be a better version of yourself. I have known Dr. Troy for several years now, and whilst we have an ocean between us, he still inspires. What he learned from his mother, we all need to learn and use her wisdom to make us a better version of ourselves. We are all in this together, let's support each other, be kind, and help each other as others helped us."

—MARLENE SHIELS
Officer of the British Empire (OBE) & Chief Executive Officer, Capital Credit Union

"I have worked with Dr. Troy Hall (a.k.a. "Dr. Troy") for over a decade; therefore, I can personally attest to his extraordinary leadership qualities as an intentional and impactful influencer. This work extracts from an unshakable foundation of principles that harnesses the power to encourage its reader to dig beyond a superficial level to a deeper internal level of understanding towards leadership."

—CRISSY ORTIZ, PHD
Professor & Founder of the Autism Platform Project

"This book is not only packed with leadership wisdom, but it's also a fun read! I love how Dr. Troy paints pictures of his beloved mom and their life in a small town. I could even envision an impactful, heartwarming movie coming out of *Fanny Rules*! You owe it to your leadership vision to read this book."

—THOMAS HEATH
Author, Speaker, Coach & Award-Winning Playwright

"To different degrees, we are all shaped by our childhood experiences and the lessons we learn from our parents, grandparents, teachers, and other influential people in our lives. In his new book, *Fanny Rules*, Dr. Troy describes—in a very relatable way—the lessons learned from his mother, Frances Rose Hosner (nicknamed Fanny). Fanny may not have been the CEO of a Fortune 500 company, but she understood how to lead like she was. Her emotional intelligence quotient (as we might say these days) was clearly advanced, and she understood—as Troy describes—that people respond better when you serve them honey to drink and not vinegar! She also knew a good saying when she heard one, and I took away so many sayings from this book that served as a reminder to me of what makes good leaders great, including that "the ladder of success goes both ways." The nine lessons described in the book became the foundation for Dr. Troy's strong leadership principles and attributes and collectively serve as a perfect extension of his previous book, *Cohesion Culture: Proven Principles to Retain Your Top Talent*. These lessons can be used to guide and develop the culture of any organization, and I am convinced that not only will you thoroughly enjoy reading this book, but you will take from it a set of leadership lessons that will serve you (and your organization) well."

—MARK SIEVEWRIGHT
Founder and CEO, Sievewright & Associate, FinTech Board Advisor, Author of *Digital Life*

"Fanny's rules are more than just mere talking points. They are the cornerstones of the foundation for the incredible leader, Dr. Troy Hall. I look forward to sharing *Fanny Rules* and these principles with everyone for two reasons. First, Fanny was a remarkable lady with great leadership insight. Secondly, part of the proceeds of the book will benefit the Alzheimer's Association. My family has spent decades caring for loved ones afflicted with this disease."

—BEN-JAMIN TOY
Team Building Expert, Global Facilitator, Chief Executive Officer of On Purpose Adventures

Fanny Rules:
A Mother's Leadership Lessons that Never Grow Old

By Dr. Troy Hall

© Copyright 2021 Dr. Troy Hall

ISBN 978-1-64663-383-8

REVIEW COPY: This is an advanced printing subject to corrections and revisions.

Published by

◣ köehlerbooks™

3705 Shore Drive
Virginia Beach, VA 23455
800−435−4811
www.koehlerbooks.com

FANNY RULES

A Mother's Leadership
LESSONS THAT NEVER GROW OLD

DR. TROY HALL

VIRGINIA BEACH
CAPE CHARLES

DEDICATION

To my dear wife, Vickie.

Thank you for the countless hours of support during many crazy work adventures and scholastic endeavors. You never complained when I left you all alone to pick up my slack of household responsibilities. You were with me through every step of my Bachelor's, MBA, and PhD programs as well as the writing of three books. I appreciate your gentleness in checking in on me when long after midnight I fell asleep at the kitchen table with my head on my laptop and my hand tightly holding a cold cup of coffee. You were so sweet in helping me to bed and diligent in making sure I was up the next morning and off to work or school. Just as you cared tirelessly for my parents, Fanny and Slim, during the last five years of their lives, you have always cared for me with that same kind spirit.

Thank you for countless hours of listening to me talk about the lessons and proofreading manuscript version after version. Although I may have authored the book, you are still an important part of it. Words are too few to express my gratitude for supporting me in creating a living testament to Mom's teachable moments. Now *Fanny Rules: A Mother's Leadership Lessons that Never Grow Old* is a mentor guide available to future generations of leaders. Because of your efforts, Fanny's legacy lives on.

With all my love,

Troy

ACKNOWLEDGMENT

Just before taking this photo for what would be my parents' last Christmas card, Mom had a dark, distant, blank stare on her face while Dad sat there in the golf cart with his big, jolly smile. Before snapping the photo, I told Mom to get close to Dad and act like she loved him. Mom cuddled up next to Dad, looked at him with the biggest grin ever as if to say, "I sure do." Snap! This photo truly captures the essence of the love shared by my dear Fanny and Slim.

TABLE OF CONTENTS

FOREWORD

THE LOSS OF A LOVED ONE to Alzheimer's is one of the most difficult experiences a child can go through. Dr. Troy and I share the magnitude of this loss: Dr. Troy with his mother Fanny, and me with my father, Richard. We are now both allies in the fight against this disease and the devastating impact it has on families.

For the last six years, I've served as an Appointed Ambassador for Congressman Cunningham for the Alzheimer's Association. I serve on the Disabilities Board of Charleston County, regularly meet with members of the General Assembly to educate legislators about state policy, and serve on the Governor's Council on Aging. Reading *Fanny Rules* was a touching reminder of how impactful amazing leaders are in our lives and how important our advocacy is.

I am a child of the 1950s who grew up in a large family of six children, always embracing the knowledge that my parents and grandparents would surround me to keep me safe and that my role as the oldest daughter would only be rewarded by their glowing pride in everything that I accomplished. My parents raised me to be independent, self-sufficient, and impressed upon me the importance of giving back and taking care of others. I must admit, though, I could never have imagined how the role reversal that Alzheimer's would place on me would change my life and the lives of my family members.

Prior to 2003, I don't think that I had ever heard the term Alzheimer's, and I know that if I did hear it, I certainly didn't know what it meant or how it could change lives in such a fierce way.

I knew people whose family members had what they described as lapses of memory, which they suggested were due to their advancing ages, forgetting little things such as names, events, etc. When my mom told me that my dad was having some trouble, I think that I thought the same thing except he was an active sixty-eight-year-old with an unmatched zeal for life. It didn't make sense.

My family and I suggested that perhaps Dad should go to MUSC hospital in Charleston to be evaluated by the Alzheimer's Center. This is when life began to change. My mom was suffering from COPD, using oxygen most of the time, and my dad was her sweetheart, the one who took care of her every day.

Being told that Dad did show definite signs of having a disease that would one day take even his oldest memory was more than I could wrap my head and heart around. I learned that one day, even on the two drugs that were approved to handle the disease, he would likely forget my mom, me and my siblings, and our children—those he treasured—and one day he would even not know his name. I then searched everywhere to find what we would need to do to keep him safe and happy as his disease progressed and as our roles would begin to reverse.

My dad passed away in early 2018.

He was diagnosed with Alzheimer's at the age of sixty-eight, and every day we lost a little bit more of him, including the last five years when he didn't recognize his children, grandchildren, or other family members. Though he didn't know us, he continued to express love to each person he encountered and showed gratitude when things were done for him, and we were so happy to have him with us as long as we did. I think that I am like him in many ways, and I still smile when I remember that.

My dad was an enormous icon and leader in my life. The lessons he taught me resonate daily, and much of my success comes from the wisdom he bestowed upon me throughout his life.

Fanny Rules is a touching tribute to Dr. Troy's late mother, Fanny. As a business and community leader, I can tell you the lessons she shared with him ring true for everyone who wants to grow both personally and professionally. I never knew Fanny personally, but I know I would have loved her. She, like my dad, was full of wisdom, and Dr. Troy perfectly captures Fanny's brilliance in these memorable stories that are just as applicable in the backyard or the boardroom.

Alzheimer's is a cruel disease. I am happy that there are people like Dr. Troy Hall who are committed to seeing the end—the day when our friends and family members will not walk such a cruel walk. We should all be as dedicated to this effort for the memories of those we love, and for the hope that our families will not have to become the parents in their relationships with us. God bless all who fight the fight every day.

Cheryll Woods-Flowers
Alzheimer's Association Ambassador to the First District Congressman

FOLLOW
THE
LEADER

"Mom believed the way you do anything
is the way you do everything."

MOM AKA FANNY

WHEN I WAS TWELVE, I was told my mom was going to die. The news shifted my entire world on its axis and changed the course of my life.

I am a mama's boy. Yep, that's me. I make no apologies and fully accept all the rights, ridicule, and benefits bestowed as such.

It was a blessing to have a loving and caring mom in my life. In my heart, I believe one of the greatest commands is to love one another as you would love yourself. And with that, the most significant personal sacrifice is when someone lays down their life for another. Mom commanded this depth of loyalty and sacrifice. Not from a position of power, but from a place of love and influence.

My mom was fondly known by her nickname, Fanny.

Sounds unusual?

Well, it is.

Born Frances Rose Hosner on May 12, 1927, she earned the nickname Fanny while attending Lost Creek High School in Lost Creek, West Virginia. By the age of sixteen, Mom was all of ninety-eight pounds soaking wet. Her girlfriends were quite flirtatious in their day. Mom was shy, saving her affections for her beloved beanpole of a man she affectionately named "Slim." I called him "Dad."

As her friends explored their teenage sexuality, Mom remained conservative and committed to her dream of being with Slim. Gloria, Mom's best girl gal, suggested Frances "up her game" and expand her horizons beyond Slim. This, of course, required Frances to show a little fanny. The girls quickly decided the only way this ninety-eight-pound woman would ever *have* a derriere would be if they *gave* it to her. The name "Fanny" was born, and Frances Rose proudly wore the moniker until the end of her life.

Before we get too far along in the book, let me set the record straight because there is a lot of talk about Mom, and I don't want you to believe Dad had any less influence on my life. I had an incredible relationship with him, too. He was a remarkable man and the love of Mom's life, who adored and cared for her throughout their beautiful marriage. He was there right up until she took her last breath on September 12, 2012, after suffering a decade or more with Parkinson's Disease and dementia.

My parents chose the traditional roles, as did most couples married and living in the 1940s. Dad was the protector and provider. Mom served as the nurturer and caregiver. In that role, Mom imparted many life lessons—her rules for how to be a leader and conduct oneself.

For me, they live as "Fanny Rules." In this book, I have captured nine lessons that were life-changing in my world. It seemed appropriate to share these with others, particularly purpose-driven leaders, regardless of their task, title, or tenure in an organization. These lessons are for anyone who wants to be a better person and take their leadership to the next level. *Fanny Rules* reflects a common-sense approach to making each of us an exceptional person and a great leader. You may think of these rules as a form of practical leadership advice that has application from simple to complex. These rules go from the backyard to the boardroom.

In the purest form, leadership is the ability to move others into action, shape one's thoughts, and provide resources while removing obstacles. This is how a leader motivates, influences, and enables others to succeed. Mom's wisdom flowed through every inch of her small and unassuming frame. She could pack it into every square inch of anyone who got to know her and spend time with her. I was fortunate to be the recipient of Fanny's wisdom that she wanted to instill in me when her very survival was on the line.

As you read the text, "Mom" is used when I describe what she did or refer to her relationship with me. "Fanny" depicts those moments when she was in full teaching mode. Regardless, Fanny is and always will be Mom, wife, Grandma Frances, or Gma Gee to multiple generations. My purpose is to share her inspirations with a new generation that may need a little *Fanny* in their own lives.

MY HOMETOWN, THE BACKDROP

I GREW UP IN A SMALL, rural town in central West Virginia. Grandpa Hosner bought a piece of property along the main road, and the two-room house became their home. It was where John and Mary welcomed and raised their only daughter and star of this book, Frances "Fanny" Rose. Over time, the two-room wooden shack with a tin roof was expanded, and the outdoor toilet was eventually brought inside when running water was finally pumped into the house. The house oozed luxury.

With a promise for grandeur, this sleepy little village did not quite live up to being a coal mining mecca that was promised during construction. It became a lonely, forgotten town absent of commerce and manufacturing. The central hub of the town, near the one and only railroad stop, no longer housed the diner or convenience store, and even the railroad tracks were removed. I guess you can't be "from the other side of the tracks" when the tracks themselves go missing.

Our town was about 250 people deep or 251 if you count the old man who wandered up and down the streets looking for bottles or tin cans he could collect to recycle.

Small.

Rural.

Hometown America.

Only homes along a main stretch of blacktop and several dwellings "down in the hollers" remained once the coal and railroad companies pulled out. Hollers are the hillbilly version of what suburban folks call cul-de-sacs. Once you travel down the dirt road, the only way to get back out is to turn around and head out the same way you came in. Not sure why we called them hollers other than I can recall Dad's mom, Grandma Goldie, saying that back in the 1920s, folks didn't have phones and to get their attention, the first neighbor had to "holler" to the next and so on until they got the attention of the person they wanted to see. I am convinced this is an urban, er...hillbilly legend for sure.

Some of the most wonderful people I know today still live in this small, homogenous community. Of those in my little hood, education was not always top of mind. Although Mom finished high school, Dad only completed eighth grade. He earned his street smarts and mechanic skills serving as a grease-monkey Army private during World War II.

These quirky and well-grounded people created a wonderful bond of belonging that made my home safe and welcoming. It was special. With some exception on Dad's part, they believed in following the Golden Rule and treating people kindly and with dignity. Everyone knew my parents, which made it extremely difficult for me to get away with anything, even if I'd wanted to.

We had a post office that placed our mail in individual boxes with number-lock combinations. The local fire department had one truck and was in a building next to a big field perfect for the annual carnival. But our town lacked a public library. Sadly, even the local gas station, grocery store, and school that housed all grades from K-12 closed just after I completed sixth grade. We could have really used a library with all the closings, as everyone suddenly had a lot of free time on their hands.

We can't forget the two main buildings in town. On Saturday, people frequented the local beer garden (West Virginia slang for the pub) to drown out their sorrows after a full week of working or hoping to work. On Sundays, the Methodist church offered refuge for people asking God to drown out the sorrows the liquor had missed.

Like any true southerner, we got gussied up and sat in our favorite pew on Sundays. Mom would whisper to me when the collection plate passed, "Boy, just remember poor is a condition of the pocketbook, not the heart." And with a bow of the head, she would ante up this week's offering and thank Jesus for the blessing.

Yes, some roughnecks loitered, looted, and lived it up just a little too much. For some reason, these rough housers didn't bother our family. Even though I did not understand it at the time, I now know it was because my parents treated them with a level of respect. They didn't try to make them wrong when holding them accountable for their actions. The guys still liked to hang out with Dad in his favorite retreat: the garage. Dad would tinker with their cars and motorbikes, finding some way to get them back on the streets again. Mom would often join them and offer some freshly baked treats. We didn't have a lot to eat, but somehow Mom seemed to find something to offer anyone who stopped by to visit. I think one of the best leadership qualities I learned was to see the good in people.

To try at least.

Well, not always.

Mostly.

LIFE AS I KNOW IT ENDS, THE RULES BEGIN

I WILL NEVER FORGET when Mom and Dad shared the heartbreaking news with their two children. My twelve-year-old ears could hardly comprehend the words.

It's not good.

It's cancer.

It's breast cancer.

To say the news was devastating is an understatement. My sister, nine years older than me, had run away from home, and if she had known what was going on, she would have surely hurried home. When she did return after Mom's recuperation, her guilt was so grave that after that, my sister never missed a day talking to Mom from her return until the day my sister died in 2003.

My brother, three years younger than me, was sheltered from what was happening. However, he must have known something was going to be different. My focus remained solely on Mom. All I vividly remember about the night they told us Mom was sick was crying in my bed, thinking, "Mom is gonna die."

In the 1960s, the primary and recommended treatment for cancer was radical surgery, meaning her surgeons would do their best to extract anything (muscle or tissue) that was possibly affected by the cancer spreading through her body. From my perspective, the hospital was a lonely place. A cold place where people usually go to die.

It was scary.

It was not a place for a mom.

It was not a place for MY mom.

Although this horrible situation was looming over her head, Mom made it clear that with each and every day, we have life.

We have opportunities.

We have choices.

Those choices have consequences.

People can look for the good in others or dwell on the bad. Fanny had a positive outlook on life, and very little got her down and out. Even a cancer diagnosis didn't keep her down.

Because Mom was the nurturer, she made the choice to delay treatment until the school year ended. During the months preceding her surgery, Mom taught me how to clean, wash clothes, shop for food, cook, and write checks. As my training progressed, her health declined. I handled many of the household chores after school, as Mom was simply too weak.

During one trip to the grocery store, I can vividly remember Mom instructing me to write my first check at the checkout counter. The young clerk immediately told Mom that I wasn't allowed to.

Mom smiled at the cashier, didn't argue, and nodded to me to continue. When I got to the signature line, she took the check, signed it, presented it for payment, and asked, "Did he fill it out correctly?" Sheepishly, the clerk accepted the check, bagged the groceries, and called for someone to walk us to the car.

This is how Fanny taught me to be a leader. She would often tell me that people responded much better when served honey to drink than vinegar. Fanny said, "There's no pride in telling other people they are wrong, shaming them in public, or making them feel small. Help them be better. Stand tall, and they will stand with you." That's just how she lived her life. Always thinking of others and how they would feel, even though she had every reason to be nasty or angry.

Cancer sucks.

Cancer is the ultimate excuse to become the worst version of yourself.

Cancer hadn't heard Fanny's rules yet.

Mom was battling for her life. I don't know how she did it. Somehow, someway, she would consistently make the choice for character regardless of circumstance.

Mom may not have been the leader of a multibillion-dollar company, yet she knew very well how to lead like she was the Chief Executive Officer. With clear conviction, Mom knew that the actions and behaviors of a person defines who they would become and how others would see and relate to them.

Reflecting back on this lesson as an adult, that is when I first recognized the level of my mom's resilience through leadership. Maybe the shock of hearing the news and translating it to death prompted me to grow up a little faster than others my age. One thing I know for sure was that Fanny refused to be defined by her circumstances. She believed in the power of choice, and today it is why I tell my grandkids, "Choices define your character, not circumstances."

BEDSIDE WISDOM

IN THE MONTHS following Mom's surgery, it was my responsibility to handle all the tasks she had trained me to do. Friends of the family took care of my brother, so I only had to tend to the house, Dad, and Mom.

Cleaning meant more than sweeping the middle of the floor and dusting around objects. It meant cleaning the surface of the furniture both around and underneath whatever was sitting on the tables. It meant getting on my hands and knees to find those hidden dust bunnies in the corners. Detailing those corners shaped my discipline, attention to detail, and accountability. Mom believed that the way you do anything is the way you do everything. Fanny taught me that anyone can sweep in the middle. It's the easy part. Fanny would say,

"A person who cares about their job will do what's needed even if it's hard.

These folks know how to take it to the corners."

I liked taking care of Dad, too. Earlier in my childhood, I can remember often waking up to the sound of Mom and Dad sitting at the kitchen table whispering and sharing an occasional laugh. I tried so hard to hear from my bedroom but never quite made out their conversations. I would just lay there, quiet as could be, never wanting to let on that I could even faintly hear them. It was a comforting time and a wonderful memory to cherish. Before too long, I would hear the front door latch. The next thing I knew Mom was calling my name to wake me up for school.

Getting up early and spending time with Dad was so special. Every weekday was like clockwork. He would awake around six a.m. and in thirty minutes be ready for the day and sit at the kitchen table. I still have fond memories of sharing dinner with lively conversations around the shiny chrome table with a yellow laminate top and brightly colored yellow, plastic-covered chairs.

Dad ate his breakfast: a single sunny-side-up egg, two pieces of buttered toast, and a cup of hot, black coffee. We would talk until it was time for him to leave for work. At the door, I handed him his lunch pail packed with all his favorites, just like Mom taught me to do.

My time with Mom was spent by her bedside. I helped her to the restroom, made sure her bandages were clean, fed her, and tucked the covers up to her chin. Sometimes she would shiver, and I would add another quilt to warm her up. Cancer is cold.

Although Mom never traveled internationally, she has unknowingly been a source of global impact through her legacy. Fanny taught me about cultural diversity and inclusion while at her bedside. She taught me why it is important not to make rash judgments about people based on their outward appearance. She told me to wait until they revealed the inside, then I would know what kind of person they were and whether I would include them in my trusted counsel of wise voices.

Mom nurtured and cared for me in ways I never expected and certainly at times did not deserve. She beat the odds that were given to her with her diagnosis and went on to live another forty-three years. Mom was a humble servant of God who instilled in me daily doses of life lessons, a process that was accelerated when her diagnosis was given.

Fanny was wife to Slim for sixty-five years, mother of three, Grandma Frances or Gma Gee to seven, and great-grandma to eleven. My parents loved nicknames and wore the names Slim and Fanny as badges of honor. In fact, most people either didn't know or had forgotten their real names, Troy and Frances. They were so good about relationships, too, that people could be formal and informal with them at the same time. I can remember Dad saying, "You can call me anything you like, just don't call me too late for dinner."

Slim and Fanny celebrated people, life, and created the perfect home of cohesion before I even knew what that word meant. In that space, I felt the truest sense of being loved—a special place where I knew I belonged. They honored me with value and respected my contributions to finding solutions for even the simplest of decisions—what to have for dinner, how to rearrange a room, or what we could make for Grandma Goldie at Christmas—all included my input. We shared mutual respect, dignity for all humankind, and banded together in adversity and good times. These life lessons, *Fanny Rules*, have carried with me through the course of my life.

Through these great tidbits of wisdom, her teachable moments, Fanny instilled in me the value of investing in others. She helped me understand the importance of not judging others too harshly or quickly when they did not look or act like me. I can still hear her voice, "Give people a second chance." Her bedside wisdom gave me a first glimpse into the real value of mentoring and how it would shape me and the choices I would make in my personal and professional life. Parents have this wonderful opportunity to be our teachers, nourishers, caregivers, providers, and protectors when they choose to be. Some children are not so lucky to have a "Slim and Fanny" in their lives, but for me, my parents were the first mentors I ever had. For that, I am eternally grateful.

Mom never lost sight of her plan to make her own choices, not based upon circumstance, but based upon will. Not sure if she would survive, that woman spent hours and hours pouring every ounce of Mom wisdom into me that she had the strength to handle. From bedside to armchair, these nine *rules* are the nuggets of wisdom that changed the course of my life.

Didn't Yo Fanny Teach Ya?

"You don't have to know everything. You just need to be teachable."

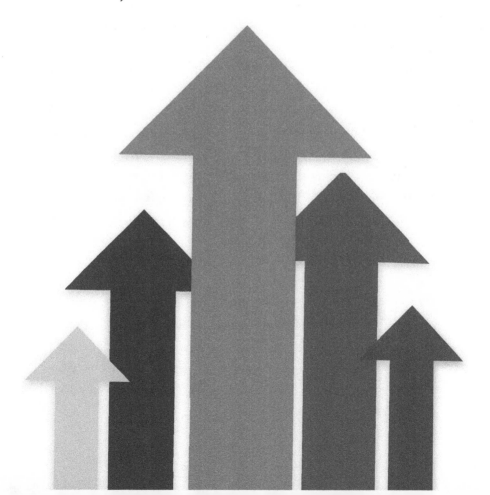

WHEN LEADERS THINK THEY KNOW EVERYTHING, THAT'S WHEN THE TROUBLE STARTS.

LEADERS WITH A KNOW-IT-ALL ATTITUDE have missed out on what "yo' mama" (in this case yo' Fanny) should have taught them. It's simply amazing to witness people failing to practice even the most reasonably expected forms of common sense and common courtesies. Fanny and Slim gave us strict instructions when we were playing in the front yard, or sitting on the porch, to be the first person to speak when others walk by. This would show respect and extend trust.

Back in the early 1960s, people in these parts of West "by God" Virginia didn't even lock their doors at night. It was a simple, laid back time when trust and honor were more common than trying to get over on someone else or "cheat them out of their due," as Dad would say. The screen door and all the windows would be left open to let in the cool mountain breeze that blew after the sun went down. You slept unencumbered from the worry of unwanted intruders while nestled deep under the handmade quilts passed down from generation to generation. The beds were a little lumpy, but Mom held to the mantra of being grateful and showing gratitude in all ways for all things big or small. Fanny would say, "If you don't like what you have, then just remember: What the good Lord giveth, He can easily take away. And, if you're not respectful, I'll be sure to claim the rest of what he leaves behind just to make sure you remember to count those blessings."

At times, I wish to retreat to those simpler days. There was this air of informality and unbridled trust. It was a simple time of welcoming strangers into one's home and sharing lemonade and a homemade sugar cookie topped with green-colored buttercream icing. Like many of life's little treasures, no one knows how good they have it, until it's gone.

I would often ask myself, "Why was it so important to be first at speaking to those who passed by?" I wasn't allowed to be first in line for ice cream treats—I had to wait my turn. It seemed silly to wait if you could hurry up and beat the other kids to the front of the line. Besides, it was fun to jump in front of Greg and Pam. They were my friends and surely didn't mind. It was just a game.

With Fanny, every opportunity was a life lesson—a teachable moment—those special times when you provide insight and let folks in on the secret of what is behind Door #2. It wasn't a lecture as if you did something wrong. It was more of a mentoring conversation with a tweak. Just enough of a slight change in my thinking that gave me a new perspective. You could think of it sort of like making an adjustment to a high-performance engine running on a race track. When it gets to the pit stop, the goal is for the pitsters to make minor changes to allow the engine to optimally perform when it goes back on the track. It's not about breaking down the engine and rebuilding it. It's about fine-tuning and operating with finesse.

Speaking first was a sign of respect. Fanny said it was how people should be treated. Fanny excelled at cultivating, nurturing, and sustaining long-term relationships. She knew it is important to be teachable, too, because that mindset fuels one's desire to learn and grow. The real magic in being a leader is how you apply the knowledge you gain along the way with how you treat people. It's not one or the other.

→ HAVE THE WILLINGNESS TO BE WRONG TO FURTHER WHAT IS RIGHT

THE BEST WINS ARE WON with passion and not position. As a young boy, it took quite a while to wrap my head around this concept. How in the world does that even make any sense? Who wants to be wrong? Of course I want to be right. Who doesn't? Certainly, this does not apply to Jesus, as He is always right. I'm not Him, so you get the point. It's confusing because every time I go into an argument, I expect to win.

Be right.

Perfecto.

Victorious.

Fanny had a different perspective in mind. It involved understanding that the *right* may start with the *wrong*. Sometimes you plant yourself so firmly on an issue it's like your feet are trapped in cement. You may want to move, but you can't. Stuck. Stubborn. It's not about being right or wrong or giving up the passion for what you believe in. Allowing yourself to be wrong tempers passion with empathy and the possibility a person may not know everything. This approach may open the door to finding an idea you never expected.

How do I get in touch with these feelings?

Can I feel another person's joy or pain?

Do I know what it's like to walk in another person's shoes?

We've all heard the metaphorical application of the rudimentary concept of how you show compassion and grace to another individual by proverbially imagining what it's like walking in step with their life. Compassion consists of the gentle actions and kindness extended to another by showing respect and honoring cultural norms, standards, rituals, and traditions. Grace is the unmerited favor another receives for no reason other than it is given as a gift without deserving, trading, or bartering for it.

From Fanny's perspective, beliefs could be upheld, but they had to be based upon the truth. Ground truth is real. It is not some loosely interpreted version of someone's reality that may not be based on fact at all. Assertions and claims not founded on facts are called opinions, ungrounded beliefs that people wield around like the sword of truth. Everyone has an opinion. Dad said everyone has opinions and some other body part, too, but that didn't make them *right*. Since this book is PG-rated, I'll leave it up to your imagination to fill in the blank of Dad's more colorful expression of a body part that rhymes with "class."

When beliefs are based on facts and verified truths and balanced with emotion, they become tenets, which can ground attitudes and behaviors for generations to come. Leaders who manage their emotional intelligence are in a position to use feelings combined with facts to advance resolutions towards the desired common ground.

This is the wisdom from a woman who graduated high school and only ever worked outside the house for three months in Washington, DC, as a switchboard operator—a story I'll share with you on another day. It took me a college degree, master's in business administration, and a PhD to understand why people make decisions using both facts and emotions. The quantifiable data provides information to evaluate the economics of a choice, while the qualitative side allows for interpretation based on feelings and emotions. Therefore, good decision-making takes both facts and emotions into account and consideration. It's what is commonly referred to today as bringing together art and science.

When it came to being teachable, Fanny felt it important to listen to what others had to say, especially those one trusted. This was more than just getting two sides to a story. It was gaining insight into the cultural influences that shaped a person's interpretation of their world and others around them. "Don't judge from the outside," she would say. "Wait until the person reveals what is inside them, then you'll know who they *really* are."

Fanny based her idea of "right" on two fundamental teachings: 1) the Golden Rule and 2) the Greatest Commandment. The Golden Rule is treating others as you want to be treated, while the Greatest Commandment is to love God with all your heart, with all your mind, with all your soul, and then love your neighbor in the same way. It wasn't about winning a debate with facts, fancy sentences, and eloquent speech. It was basing "right" on common decency and mutual respect.

Fanny helped me find that space where I could give myself permission to have the mindset to be wrong to further what is right.

Looking at right and wrong through a transformative leadership lens, today I have a whole new perspective of right and wrong. As a mentor, I set my first teachable moment with every mentee as "You don't have to know everything, you just need to be teachable." I encourage them to seek new information, gain perspective, and ask questions to help with interpretation, integration, and implementation of who they are and what they want to do.

"Give yourself some room," I could hear Fanny say. "Why box yourself into a space only to find out the box is too small?" My interpretation of what she was saying is don't be so rigid that your ego gets in the way of modifying your stance because you are worried about how you might look.

Being teachable requires you to have the ability to accept information from different viewpoints and cultural backgrounds and have an open box without traditional walls or barriers. Allow insight and information to help shape the decisions and innovative solutions you suggest, lead, and put in place. Being of a mindset that accepts what others believe as their truth without making the person wrong is more of an art than science.

Respect.

Feel.

Understand.

In other words, one can respect and understand how a person feels, how they think, what shaped their views, and how all of this impacts their reaction to the world today, yet it does not mean agreement. It only means understanding. That's the value of an open mind and an open box. Fanny often chuckled when people would say, "Think outside the box." She countered, "What if the answer *is* the box?"

Remember the cashier mentioned in the Introduction, *Follow the Leader*? She didn't think it was right for me to write a check at such a young age. Mom knew the cashier. She knew her momma, daddy, and grandparents, the manager, assistant manager, floor supervisor, and most of the other folks working at the store. But Fanny did not show herself as better or immediately disproving of the cashier's behavior. After I had written the check, Fanny asked, "Did he fill it out correctly?" Fanny was willing to be wrong to further what was right.

It wasn't about making the cashier feel wrong, embarrassed, or ashamed. It wasn't about Mom asserting her authority trying to improperly intimidate the cashier by throwing out all the important names she knew. Fanny wanted the cashier to have a teachable moment and a learning lesson filled with self-discovery. Fanny knew that if the cashier could feel good about what she was being taught, then the opportunity for the cashier to learn and grow would be increased. The cashier entered the conversation wanting to be right. Banking was very formal in those days. Every line of the check had to be properly completed because (believe it or not) someone at the bank reviewed every single check for accuracy. The proofers pulled signature cards to ensure the signer was fully authorized to make the transaction before releasing payment. And the cashier's number one job was to handle the cash and collect the payment.

While the cashier attempted to follow a rule, she was narrow in her thinking. The cashier wasn't willing to be wrong. She assumed the entire check had to be handwritten by the signer. Not being open to how one can apply norms and standards can create an experience that polarizes people and forces the situation into a battle of wits or fists.

In a very caring way, Fanny refrained from using authoritative power to make her point. When the leader uses authoritative power, others affected by it are ruled from a heavy hand. There isn't anything wrong with using authoritative power as long as the leader understands that wielding authority in this manner is to efficiently get things done, follow established policies, protocol, or standards, or to bring order to chaos. Power should never be used to oppress or victimize another living creature.

In the story of Fanny and the Cashier, she used influential power and empowered the cashier to look at her behavior and modify it. Not because Fanny said so, but because it was the right thing to do. Fanny showed the cashier that her box just wasn't big enough. It's funny how when you are open to being wrong, you actually move closer to what is right. It means you are receptive to new ideas, viewpoints, and information you did not know or have access to. And there are times when knowing something isn't enough. We must put the learning into action so that knowledge becomes wisdom.

→ LEARN IT ALL VS. KNOW IT ALL

MOM ENCOURAGED ME to be a sponge and soak up all the knowledge I could. She suggested being a rock when you need to decide if the information was valuable to use or not. She was very careful to not use the words "wisdom" and "knowledge" interchangeably. It wasn't for some time that I understood the difference between wisdom and knowledge and how to apply the sponge and rock concept effectively. Hang in there; the meaning of wisdom and knowledge comes later in the story.

In school, I was a good student. My edge over some of the other students was my ability to easily retain and recall information I saw or read. I learned quickly and was able to comprehend complex topics with little supervision. For some reason, my brain was able to internalize concepts and use them in a very practical way.

The stage was set. Entering the scene is the character Horshack from the 1975-1979 TV series *Welcome Back Kotter*. For those of you unfamiliar with the show, you will more than likely be able to identify this type of character from your past school experiences. Horshack wanted his fellow classmates to know how much he knew. When Mr. Kotter, the teacher, asked a question, Horshack would immediately raise his hand up and down and shout with enthusiasm, "Ooh. Ooh. Pick me. Pick me."

Pitifully transparent.

Painful, maybe even disturbing.

I was a Horshack.

Part of the after-school routine would be to share my day's experiences with Mom. She was always attentive and wanted to hear everything that happened during the day. Never taking "nothing" as an acceptable response when asked, "What happened today?" I knew I better ante up something good or it was going to be a long time before getting a snack and retreating to watch *Match Game* or *Hollywood Squares* on TV.

After a few weeks of sharing my stellar "Horshack" moments, Mom asked me to help her dry the dishes. Not sure why it was so important to do that when I was going to miss Paul Lynde making snide remarks for the block on the Hollywood version of Tic-Tac-Toe. Reluctantly, I picked up the dish cloth to hurry the chore of drying the dishes and helping to set the table. As Fanny asked me questions this time, they were more direct and with purpose than her more casual approach in previous days.

Not making eye contact, she continued to dig deeper. In a true mentoring fashion, Fanny helped me realize that it's okay to know a lot of information. One should never be embarrassed or hide their intellect. The teachable moment was to understand that one's smarts don't have to be shoved in people's faces.

I could relax a little.

Let others shine.

See what they knew.

Until that discussion, I hadn't realized that my exuberance of wanting to answer the questions kept others from sharing what they knew, thus stifling the dynamic exchange of information between people that promotes learning and enlightenment. I was inhibiting indirect learning, and I was also negatively impacting my ability to learn from others. I didn't have to let everyone know I was smart.

(In full disclosure, I was the kid who knew where the library was well before finding the gymnasium.)

For me, being smart was my way of being good at something. Because I wasn't proficient in sports, I used my intellect to compensate for lacking the talent to throw a football or sink a three-pointer.

It seemed so important to show up in front of the line. Couldn't be first to get the ice cream, but I could be first at buzzing in and clearing the *Jeopardy!* category of "I'll take *Topics that Make Me Look Smart* for $500, Alex." Why was this lesson conducted while drying dishes? Fanny knew that I tended to become defensive when questioned eye to eye or the discussion was intense or emotional. It had something to do with the Alpha Male Syndrome.

How in the world did my mom know this stuff? She used drying dishes as a way to keep me from becoming overly defensive and allowing my emotions to relax. This allowed my brain to be open, hear what she had to say, and process it without feeling as though I was being made wrong.

Subtle.

Self-discovery.

Fanny was brilliant.

Before the lesson was completely over, Fanny reminded me, "God gave you two ears and one mouth." This was on purpose. It is so you will do twice as much listening as talking. Listening is important in our ability to learn. When hearing through the auditory channel, the mind is actively engaged in a process of collecting data for the purpose of storing it for future use. While collecting this information, the brain acts like a sponge. Before wringing out the sponge to transfer all the knowledge into storage, speech is engaged. While speaking, the brain is taking a break from collecting and is now trying to determine where to store the newly acquired data, or if it should even be stored at all.

This was the day Fanny taught me the difference between knowledge and wisdom. Knowledge is what you learn. It's the information you acquire from reading, hearing, or what is learned from observing the behaviors of others. Wisdom is putting what you have read, heard, felt, tasted, or seen into action. It's the interpretation of learning that is fully integrated and modeled into what you know.

Knowledge by itself is not power. If not careful, one can turn a love for learning into becoming a hoarder of information, keeping knowledge for oneself and finding value in just having it. When knowledge has power, wisdom is present. All in all, it was a valuable lesson in learning why and how to become a *Dr. Learn-It-All* instead of a *Mr. Know-It-All.*

→ LEADERS WHO "HAVE GOT THIS" NEED MORE TEACHABLE MOMENTS

Teachability is the first attribute of an effective leader, especially one focused on building cohesive teams. In Act One of my book *Cohesion Culture: Proven Principles to Retain Your Top Talent,* one important aspect of being the leader means adhering to seven effective attributes.

1. Teachable.
2. Compassion.
3. Grace.
4. Humility.
5. Truth-seeking.
6. Intentionality.
7. Peacemaking.

Selecting teachability as the first to focus on is a purposeful choice. Being teachable sets the tone for how one's mindset is open to processing information and arriving at thoughts that impact decisions and actions. It's not just the information that matters. It's how the leader processes it and what information is meaningful and worthy to be retained and used. Just as all nine rules work in tandem, so do the seven attributes. Each can stand on their own. From time to time, one attribute may be more useful in a situation than another, but the bonus power is when they are used together.

When it comes to what leaders let into their minds, it matters. The quality of the input affects the quality of the output. As the leader is hungry for information, it's important to be careful what the leader's brain consumes. This cautionary advice directs the leader to view information and knowledge from both a discerning nature and an intuitively minded perspective.

Being an authority on a topic is not a problem. Where it goes awry is when the leader is so full of himself, he has no room to learn anything else. This leader thinks he already knows everything and has no space or tolerance for anyone else, no other ideas allowed. Know-it-alls lead with ego, and that overbearing personality trait gets in the way. There is no shame in not knowing. Pretending to be "on top of the game" when in fact they are not is shameful. Leaders should show how to be authentic or genuine. You either know it or you own up to not knowing. And when you don't know, then go back and learn more.

The "have got this" type of leaders are not characteristic of following Transformative Principles such as aspiring vision and teaching it, being good with people, creating trusted environments, or practicing self-awareness. They are focused on transaction versus transformation, with their egos telling them that not knowing is a sign of weakness. These types of leaders are often weak and ineffective because they are in essence pretenders. They simply are not teachable.

Leaders of transformation are good social architects, meaning they are smart in relating and dealing with others. These leaders create a trusted environment operating with high levels of moral, ethical, and legal behavior topped off with a strong desire to earn the respect of others. Finally, transformative leaders adopt and practice self-regard, which is the ability to evaluate their actions, guard personal emotions, and interpret others' feelings. Through the concern for others and their well-being, being smart with people, creating trust, and practicing self-regard, leaders use these principles to bring about cohesive and high-performing work environments.

"Doing it myself" is not a new concept. In fact, I remember as a child being a little stubborn (shock face) and oftentimes telling Mom that I could do it on my own.

Didn't need her help.

Just watch me.

I am a big boy now.

Wanting to assert my independence and autonomy was not the problem; not having the proper information or experience to handle the situation was. My lack of maturity impacted my ability to understand that getting a little help was still a good thing. Fanny said, "Asking for help is a sign of confidence, not weakness."

Just think what it would be like to try and ride a bike without training wheels. Or to hit a baseball without first using a T-stand. Becoming proficient at a skill or mastering an academic discipline requires rigorous effort to learn, the drive to apply it, and undying commitment to succeed. There is no shame in asking for or getting some help.

Leaders who claim to know everything fail the teachability test. They forge forward fully thinking they have it handled and are in control. Unteachable leaders think they already know the very best way to do something, and once their mind is made up, there is no changing it. The reality is that leaders who fail to be good learners are not willing to be wrong to further what is right. They haven't learned the difference between knowledge and wisdom, nor the value in allowing others to be a contributor.

Unfortunately, unteachable, "know-it-all" types simply make their mamas look bad.

TEACHABLE MOMENTS

- Have the willingness to be wrong to further what is right—fight with passion and not for position. When you get that urge to dig in your heels and remain steadfast, it is an opportunity to gut check, "Are you being convicted or just plain old stubborn?" Sometimes these two concepts get confused. People think they are holding steadfast to some standard or tenet that is grounded in truth only to find that they have been one-sided in their thinking. If you have the willingness to be wrong, then you are in a position to accept new information and further something that is right. This concept is not about being either right or wrong. It is about the willingness to further understanding and compassion without needing to be positional.

- Learn it all vs. know it all—not everyone needs to know how smart you are. Learning and knowing are two very different approaches to information. As you learn, you are gathering information and in the process being generative. Knowing implies you have nothing to learn. Being in the state of discovery promotes one's ability to be adaptive, experimental, diverse-minded, and good stewards of resources.

- Leaders who "have got this" need more teachable moments—thinking you have to know or do everything yourself can get in the way of true, unbridled success.

For your free *Fanny Rules* Teachable Moments Journal go to https://drtroyhall.com/documents/fannyrulesjournal.pdf.

MENTORING LESSONS FOR RULE ONE: TEACHABLE

When working with your Mentor, reflect on the three teachable moments included in Rule One: Teachable. It is a good practice to prepare for each mentoring session by reflecting on the questions before the session. While engaged in the process of learning, ask yourself these three questions:

1. What's the source of the information I am about to trust?
2. Does "what I am hearing" make sense?
3. How can I apply what I am learning?

During the session, discuss the last time you were in an argument and ask:

1. What was the topic or issue?
2. Who was involved?
3. If you felt you were right, what led you to that conclusion?
4. Could you have been wrong to further what is right?
5. How could this have helped in the understanding and compassion for the other person's point of view?

SPACE PANTS, STEP LADDERS and HONKING HORNS

"If you speak words of affirmation, you will never be misquoted."

MOM KNEW A GOOD SAYING WHEN SHE HEARD ONE.

QUITE OFTEN, WHEN I WAS PICKING on my brother, or criticizing someone at school, Fanny would look up from what she was doing and remind me, "If you cannot say anything nice, don't say anything at all." Mom instilled in me the importance of looking beyond the surface and finding something that you liked about another person. Not a simple compliment about hair or clothes—something about who they are. "It's about what's inside," she'd say. "Affirm the person with a genuine and thoughtful comment." Affirmation was an essential foundation in how we were expected to treat people.

Mom did not believe in gossip, bullying, and talking behind one's back. She also felt it was important to stand up for oneself. Do it respectfully, even if you didn't believe the other person was deserving. When I came home complaining about occasional "backstabbing" mishaps at school, Fanny would get real close and whisper, "That's a good thing." I'd look at her with an inquisitive face. "It means if they are talking about you, then they are leaving someone else alone." Then she'd give a quick laugh and make sure it wasn't too serious. Mom stood up for us anytime she needed to but encouraged us to stand up for ourselves. However, for most of these situations, "Turn the other cheek," was Fanny's mantra.

We had a saying around the house: "Treat people right." It meant that no matter what status a person had in life, show them respect. Mom expected us to have manners and, more importantly, show them. Make people feel that each one of them is the most crucial person in the room. Smile and be pleasant. Make eye contact, but don't stare them down. Open the door for someone else. Let those older than you enter the room first. Fanny did not want us to be bashful when speaking to people. "I gave you a name, so when someone asks what it is, say it loudly enough for them to hear it. Then ask them their name."

Speak clearly.

Ask people about themselves.

Encourage them to talk.

Mom often joked that when people tell you about themselves, they are talking about their favorite subject, which always made me smile. Fanny was quick to point out that people respond more favorably with something sweet than with a sour tart. After all, we all know that a spoonful of sugar helps the medicine go down, and drinking honey is more preferred to that of vinegar. She said you don't want a lousy aftertaste left in someone's mouth once you've left the room. Therefore, her best advice, "If you speak words of affirmation, you will never be misquoted."

Mom was a stickler for speaking kindly and telling the truth. There was no place for a liar or even trying to get away with a "half lie." When you half lie, it means you leave out information to put yourself in a better light. It's not that you told a complete lie; you just left out a particular detail that you didn't want others to know because it made you look bad.

Mom had no tolerance for lying. I can tell you from personal experience that telling the truth was much better than trying to misrepresent it. Now, she did not believe in capital punishment but did subscribe to the concept that a little motivation on the behind might be just what the doctor ordered. With Mom, do not tell a:

Somewhat lie.

Casual lie.

Half lie.

Or "that" kinda big ol' lie.

When you lied, you suffered the consequences of a *lecture*, not just what we called a "talking to." It involved something that could make an impression. Let's just call it a *Fanny*-lecture.

WE ALL PUT OUR PANTS ON
ONE LEG AT A TIME

THE STRANGEST ADAGES bring forth the best lessons. Mom learned many of these new sayings from her time living through the Great Depression and World War II. During those two dramatic life experiences, she learned how important it was to build relationships. Everyone was fighting for their share of supplies. Sometimes you found yourself in the position of being vulnerable and waiting for the generosity of another person for food, shelter, or transportation.

Here is how I first learned about "putting on your pants" and what it meant as a foundational premise of treating people. Mom had to run some "special" errands in the big city with the fancy buildings, restaurants, and the Woolworth's department store. My brother was playing at Grandma Goldie's house, which was four doors down the blacktop road from our house. Mom and I got dressed like we were going to church, but it was Thursday, and church was just up the street, not over thirty miles away. It didn't matter to me because I loved going on long car rides, and it was especially lovely spending time with Mom.

Mom was definitely in a hurry to get started, and she even drove a little faster than usual on this trip. We parked at a meter and began checking one task after the other off our list. Mom was in full gait walking down the sidewalk, and my little legs found it hard to keep up. As we moved through the list, I noticed Mom kept checking her watch. At precisely three o'clock, we came to a big building on the corner of Third and Fourth Streets. To these little eyes, it seemed as though the building extended into the sky and disappeared into the clouds. Before entering, Mom looked at her reflection in the glass on the door. Then she:

Took a deep breath.

Straightened her bonnet.

Gave a slight tug on her purple jacket and checked her hair.

In a matter of seconds, before my very eyes, she transformed from hurry-up mom on a mission bent on winning a TV scavenger-hunt game show to businesswoman extraordinaire. I knew we were in a prominent building, and Mom was focused on a different kind of mission that didn't have anything to do with a game show. She was pretty secretive about the mission, and I knew better than to press for information. Mom was definitely in serious mode.

As we entered the building, I opened the door for her. Mom entered and nodded her head affirmatively. Then she gave a gentle nod and a "good day" to the man who was sweeping the floor. I followed and did the same. He smiled back at me. We went upstairs to a landing. The lady behind the desk was wearing a headset and operating a device that had bright lights that kept changing. There were several black cords and plugs that went this way and that way into the machine (a switchboard). The two women exchanged pleasant conversation as if they were old friends. I heard Mom tell the lady she had an appointment at three fifteen. Mom liked being on time. She felt that you were disrespecting the person you were meeting with if you were late.

A few minutes later, a handsomely dressed, gray-haired gentleman entered the waiting area from a private office down the hall. He welcomed Mom with a friendly greeting and a firm handshake and escorted her to his office. I sat on the brown leather couch of this large waiting area looking around at the marble floors, wood paneling, and beautiful glass chandeliers hanging from the ceiling. I was perfectly content eating my favorite treat, Smarties candy, and wondering how long Mom would be.

She finally emerged with a smile after what seemed like forever. Mom grabbed my hand to leave and again passed by the lady at the greeter's desk, who she acknowledged with a wave. The same man who was wearing a cap and dressed in a light-gray and skinny blue pin-striped jumpsuit was at the bottom of the stairs. This time he was dusting the ledge of the long row of windows with bars. Again,

Mom and the cleaning man exchanged greetings. This time, he held the door for us.

As we were driving home, Fanny shifted into *teachable moment* mode. We discussed the three people we saw that day—Mr. Leonard, the janitor; Miss Mary Ellen, the secretary; and the company president, Mr. Lowndes. Mom had regularly met these people when she cashed Dad's weekly paycheck and when she and Dad took out a small loan to buy a family car. On the day Mom and I visited the bank, I wasn't clear about the reason for the visit to the man who looked like a grandpa in the big, fancy building. However, I knew it was important because Mom never put on her Sunday best to go to the city. Her singing on the way back home signaled her delight with the meeting's outcome.

As time passed, I understood that Mom met with Mr. Lowndes because she and Dad were late on the car payment. Mom wanted to meet with the bank president face to face to extend their personal promise to pay. It was Mom's way of showing respect to him and honoring our family's financial obligations.

Mom was strict about how she treated people. My brother and I were expected to speak to everyone with kindness and to show respect through our greeting, smile, and firm handshake. To her, it didn't matter what job you held, how much money you had or didn't have, where you lived, or how educated you were. Everyone was to be treated with the same level of respect.

After returning home from our trip to the city and changing clothes, my brother was still with Grandma Goldie, so Mom and I retreated to the rockers on our front porch. We rocked and watched an occasional car pass when we gave them the customary wave. As usual, most waved back, and some even honked their horns. After taking a sip of Dr. Pepper, Mom asked, "How do you think Mr. Leonard puts his pants on?"

I loved it when she asked me questions. It was like a game. However, I preferred when Mom asked me questions that I had the answer to.

And, definitely, ones that seemed to make sense. This question was a little odd. But rest assured, she had a reason for everything.

I started rocking faster, looking all around, squirming, and trying not to make eye contact. Hey, give this kid a break. I had only met Mr. Leonard a couple of hours ago. From what I could tell, he had very long legs that seemed to fit nicely into what I thought looked like a space outfit with a very long zipper. At first, I thought it was a trick question and retorted, "He puts them on with the fly in the front." I was quite pleased with my answer and continued rocking. Even Mom chuckled.

"No," she said. "How does he physically put his pants on?" I know Mom thought that changing up the question was going to spark the correct response, but it wasn't helping. Being the type of kid that liked to show how much I knew, I was stumped. I reluctantly admitted my cluelessness and asked, "How does he put his pants on?" Fanny smiled. "One leg at a time."

There was a long pause of silence as I tried to understand what that meant. Fanny saw that I might not have fully understood, so she explained. Occasionally folks measure up one another by the type of job they hold, who they know, or what kind of car they drive. Sometimes people get confused and think that different hairstyles or body types are what make them unique. Those things make them look uniquely different, but they are just descriptors to help us distinguish people when we speak about them to someone else. What makes people special is what's on the inside.

Fanny was adamant that people's choices determined the type of person they were. Their beliefs, attitudes, and behaviors all sourced from the person's inner core. And if their core values supported the Golden Rule of treating people how you wanted to be treated, it would show up in how they treated others and how the person thought of themself.

The purpose of her visit didn't matter to me. I was more enamored with the whole experience than the details of why we went to that big, tall building. My takeaway from our trip was understanding how important it was to treat people the same regardless of whether they were the CEO, the clerk, or the janitor. Building relationships through showing kindness and giving respect would be more important than what I could have ever imagined. People remember you in a positive light based on how you treat them.

This mentoring lesson was all about ensuring that when I grew up, I would remember that people deserve to be treated fairly and with respect. After all, each of us put our pants on the same way, one leg at a time.

→ SPACE PANTS: KEEP IT IN THIS WORLD

HAVE YOU EVER SAID SOMETHING you wished you hadn't? Talking out of turn is especially tricky for a smart kid who has a quick wit and is not fully mature in his thinking. If he isn't careful, his humorous retorts can come off like a smart aleck, even though he is trying to be funny.

"Be careful what you say," Fanny cautioned. "Think before you speak. Once it's out, there's no taking it back." Well, I have had plenty of those times in my life.

Too quick on the draw.

Should have known better.

My humor is not *your* humor.

One rainy day, my brother and I were playing with our toys on the living room floor. Our ritual was to draw an imaginary line down the center of the room when we were together in the same space so we both knew to stay on our own side of the line. I took good care of my things, played with my toys one at a time, and put them neatly away when playtime was over. My brother was messy. He would wreck his cars, step on his Tinker Toys, and use crayons to add extra color to the pages of his reading books.

Although we had our differences, Mom held tightly to the concept that we were family. As such, we were taught to stick up for one another and to have each other's backs. There was no excuse that would get us out of trouble if we did not treat each other well. Fanny was very clear: "If you can't treat your brother kindly and with respect, then you aren't going to do it well with someone else." Some lessons take longer to learn.

My favorite toy, which I still have today, was Billy Blast Off—a plastic figurine of a boy astronaut. Billy stands about six inches tall, with movable arms and legs, dressed in a red, white, and blue spacesuit. Billy's outfit came complete with a helmet, movable visor, ray gun, and a matching red battery pack. The batteries operated the light on the top of a handheld ray gun when it was plugged into the side connector of the battery pack. When Billy was seated in any one of three small action vehicles, the low gear on the battery pack aligned with the matching gear on the vehicles. Billy was so cool. He was mine. All mine.

My brother knew Billy Blast Off was a special toy, yet every chance he got, he tried to play with it. I had to tell him over and over again to leave Billy alone. I wanted to tell him in the nicest way possible, but he never listened. Maybe he was listening, but certainly not complying. This really bugged me. Why would he want to play with my toys when he couldn't even take care of his own toys? It continued to make me mad every time he took Billy without my permission. I was especially protective of my astronaut buddy.

One evening, Mom called me into the other room for a minute. Upon returning, the unthinkable happened. My brother decided to have an outdoor space adventure with *my* Billy Blast Off. I never took Billy outside or let any of my friends play with him. My brother knew this. I lost control. I snatched up Billy and yelled, "You can never, never, ever touch him again. If you do, I swear I will ask God to send you to *H E double toothpicks.*"

Mom had supersonic hearing ability. It must have been her

superpower. She entered the scene, and in an instant, the commotion ceased. It was as if time stopped. You could have heard a pin drop. My brother had that "don't look at me, it was him" kind of look. My ugly, screaming face was motionless. It was as if a blast of cold air had swept into the room and froze my mouth and squished-up nose. Mom raised her eyebrow and began staring me down. Man, here comes the stink eye. Boy, was I in big trouble, even though my brother should have been punished for taking my toy. I was in trouble because I had gone off into space with a single rant that violated all the rules of treating people kindly.

Mom expected us to show respect to people, all people, and although I hated to admit it, that meant my brother, too. I knew in that instant that I had committed a multitude of sins.

Disrespected God.

Treated my brother poorly.

Devalued my self-worth.

Let my mom down.

I did apologize to him, but as they say, the deed was done. After cleaning up my portion of the play area, Mom escorted me to my room. She sat on the edge of the bed and lectured, er...talked to me about what I had said and the mean tone I had—it was inconsiderate according to our house rules. I cried. She hugged me. I didn't sleep well. It was the longest night ever. Yet I learned another valuable lesson about treating people with respect that applied to everyone, even my brother. Another teachable moment to add to my list and put into action moving forward.

Several years later, I was sixteen years old and ready to drive. Mom and Dad gave me a wallet for my birthday just so I could put my driver's license in it. Although this book is about Fanny, I can't leave out Dad. He gave me a card for my wallet and told me to always keep it with me. Dad said, "Remember, your mom and I expect you to respect the laws of the road and people you encounter along the way." For years, I kept the card with me until the edges became so tattered it fell apart. On one side, it read: "Good for one pair of Space Pants" and on the other, "For the guy who thinks his '___' is out of this world." Dad was such a kidder. He had a wonderful sense of humor and a genuine belly laugh that was contagious. He loved funny sayings like that. It was Dad's way of telling me not to get too big for my britches.

Treat people with respect.

Not better than the next person.

Put your pants on, one leg at a time.

I loved that man.

THE LADDER OF SUCCESS GOES BOTH WAYS

"IF YOU HAVE TO TEAR someone down to build yourself up, you weren't that damn good to begin with." This was part of Mom's bedside wisdom. She had no problem adding a curse word or two, mainly for effect. During those months after Mom's surgery, while tending to her, she really focused her teaching on the importance of treating people kindly and fairly. "Give them respect and earn their respect back." Mom banked on the fact that I was teachable. She believed that successful people who were respected, trusted, and admired also had excellent social skills. Mom knew that social skills would be critical to my success in both my personal and professional life. Fanny had no problem repeating lessons over and over again, especially this one. Moms have intuition when it comes to their kids—they know what's going on and what's best for them. Fanny sure did!

For days on end, we would talk about achieving goals without doing so at the expense of others. Mom wanted to make sure that I earned my way up the ladder of success, and she was confident I could do it without sacrificing my moral conviction of treating people how I would want to be treated. She was keenly aware of the unintended consequences that come with success when one's humility is not in check.

Being the type of person who did right by others and myself would require me to understand the power of my ego. Mom wanted to make sure I did not get off track and allow little wins to boost my confidence in a way that would lead to arrogance. It gets downright ugly when one's desire to be the best—to win, to win at any cost—does so at a detriment to others, and even oneself. Mom wanted me to:

Climb the ladder.

Enjoy every step.

Get to the top.

Know the cost to do so.

Fanny's teachings included many biblical wisdoms. She taught me about the ACTS of prayer: to *Acknowledge* God as the creator, *Confess* my wrongs, give *Thanks* for all I have been given, and to *Supplicate*, petitioning for the needs of others. Fanny said, "Glory goes in one direction, not left or right nor downward. Glory only goes up."

Mom knew that I was capable of more than I even knew myself. From the time I was a young boy, I had a good memory, an uncanny ability to learn at a quick rate, internalize information, and then apply it in a practical way. I was self-motivated, dependable, and a fierce competitor. She saw the making of a leader in me before I could fully comprehend what it would mean to me and my future.

While enjoying a sandwich for lunch during her recovery from cancer, Mom asked me if I knew about the Ladder to Success. Honestly, I hadn't seen one but sort of had an idea. "It's what a person climbs to get what they want from the top shelf." She smiled and said, "That's a good start."

For many days in a row, the lunchtime conversation was focused on talking about that ladder. Fanny concluded the lesson with, "Be careful who you step on while climbing to the top because you will see those same people on your way back down." To me, it was an odd way of summarizing the lesson. Yet she would repeat it over and over and over again.

In her teachings on this topic, she would also tell me that the space between the rungs of the ladder represented the various advancements I might experience in my career. The open space represented all the possibilities. The rungs symbolized the people in my life who were part of my journey and life experiences. Regardless of how people acted or reacted, Mom insisted I remember to treat people how I wanted to be treated whether they deserved it or not. She reminded me that there were still ways to achieve my goals and, when needed, to stand up for myself without disrespecting others.

In this lesson, we also discussed how I should handle my disappointment when others advanced further and faster. Instead of directing my frustration at others, Fanny encouraged me to channel my energies elsewhere. The focus should be on my choice to build a successful future and not get distracted with circumstances. Fanny suggested, "Constantly ask your bosses what you can do for them, how you can improve your performance; ask them for their advice and guidance."

Fanny continued to emphasize, "Be careful who you step on while climbing to the top because you will see those same people on your way back down." To that, I very calmly and sweetly replied, "Mom, I wasn't planning to step on anyone on my way up or down the ladder." Mom gave me her reassuring smile, drew me closer to kiss my forehead, and exhaled, "Good, now onto the next lesson. But that will be another day. I am tired now."

 ## HONKING NOT HOGGING

During a leadership workshop I conducted in Asia, a young participant asked, "Is it okay to boast about my accomplishments?" To which my response deferred to the sage advice from my dear, sweet Grandma Goldie:

"If you don't honk your own horn, don't expect someone else to do it for you. Just don't lay on it."

There's a fine line between acknowledgment and humility, which many leaders question when balancing the two. Numerous leadership studies and good common sense conclude that effective leaders espouse gratefulness and model humility. So, what can one learn from comparing these two characteristics to the conventional wisdom of Granny? Humility is not the same as passivity. First and foremost, let's clear up this point: Humility is not a sign of weakness or being passive. It's a modest opinion of how one thinks of themself. Leaders who act with humility respect other's work, do not cause harm, and give credit where credit is due. They exude confidence and competence in an area of authority-knowledge or skill set.

Humble leaders are self-efficacious and do not feel the need to boast unnecessarily about their accomplishments or actions. They see value in what they do, as well as others. Although these types of leaders are more passive about sharing their achievements does not mean they are not contributors. They are aware of their contributions and the work of others, celebrating all achievements along the way. Leaders who effectively adopt the attribute of humility let their actions speak for them while shining the light on others.

Finally, when contributions are valued, people understand their self-worth, which can lead to a sense of belonging. Fanny agreed with Grandma Goldie. Honk when you do good, just don't lay on the horn too long. In other words, it is okay to toot on occasion, just don't be that leader who becomes the braggart, dream stealer, or honor-grabbing hog. If leaders are seen as such, then they have laid on the honker for way too long.

TEACHABLE MOMENTS

- We all put our pants on one leg at a time—treat people on equal terms regardless of physical differences or backgrounds. Show respect to people regardless of their age, job, dress, the color of skin, or shape of their body. We are all human. It is a much better place when we remember that concept and put it into action. Treat people right.
- Space Pants: Keep it in this world—avoid acting like you are better than the next person. Show respect for everyone, and that includes family members.
- The ladder of success goes both ways—as you advance in your career, be considerate of those you pass along the way. If you have to tear someone down to build yourself up, you're not that good to begin with. Stepping on or over people to get ahead has life-long consequences. This doesn't mean you hold back from being your best. It means don't use others to get what you want. Earn it on your own merits.
- Honking not hogging—through humility, don't shy away from acknowledging the contributions of others, including yourself. There is nothing wrong with a little self-praise. Just keep it to a minimum. Spend more of your time building up and affirming others. Give credit where credit is due. Have confidence, not arrogance.

For your free *Fanny Rules* Teachable Moments Journal go to https://drtroyhall.com/documents/fannyrulesjournal.pdf.

MENTORING LESSONS FOR RULE TWO: TREAT OTHERS RIGHT

Observe and make notes in a journal of the following:

- When you are walking into your department or within a work area, and someone else is already in that space, who speaks first?
  - What are our thoughts about who it is or who it should be?
  - Is there a right or wrong answer?
  - Keep this within the spirit of the lesson. If you are part of a large crowd of people, this is not the ideal time to keep track. The point of the observation is bring Rule Two: Treat Others Right into perspective and challenge your thinking.
- If you're with a group of people (for example, co-workers), who goes into a building first? Who holds the door open?
- During a discussion, how often do you start with an open-ended question such as:
  - Tell me more about it...
  - Why does...
  - How can I...
  - What do you think...
- Who was the last person you affirmed? And why?
- On a scale of 1 to 10, rate yourself when it comes to:
  - Treating other people with kindness.
  - Giving and showing others respect.
  - Responding to others based on how they treated you.
- What have you discovered about yourself and how you treat people?

DON'T BOTHER COMPLAINING. AIN'T NOBODY LISTENING

"You cannot be a victor of your future if you are held captive by your past."

WHEN I FIND MYSELF COMPLAINING, MY LOVING WIFE, VICKIE, WHO I FONDLY CALL "V," OFTEN SAYS TO ME, "YOU'RE ON IT AGAIN."

SOMETIMES IT JUST FEELS GOOD to let it out. However, the secret is not letting it out to the point that others are wasted in what I call a "Volcanic Complaint Eruption." This is when I spew all my negativity, feel better, then leave others around me in the aftermath to clean up the mess. So, with the early help of Fanny and the continued support of V, I am conscious of how and when I "get on it."

A good friend of mine often said, "It's not about how many times you get *on it* that counts, it's how quickly you get *off it* that matters." Fanny's advice was, "Everyone has problems. How are you going to fix what's wrong without dragging everyone along with your ride on the Complaint Express?" Those two pieces of advice would make me stop and think of my responsibility in the matter at hand. It goes back to making choices based on character and not circumstance. Quite frankly, I can narrow down the root of my complaints as a derivative of me allowing my circumstance to control how I felt, what I said, or what action I would take.

Complaining brings us down, and when we focus on the negative, we're simply looking for who and what to blame. The flip side is that when we look for the positive, we begin to see solutions. So stay focused on what's possible, and instead of worrying about what's wrong, focus on what's right.

Effective leaders who understand and command the values of emotional intelligence approach problems with a positive mindset. Having a positive and open mindset can produce wonderful results, such as:

1. More than one solution to a problem. Remember what Fanny

said: "It's okay to look for answers outside the box, as long as you don't forget the solution may very well be the box."

2. Problems are not as complex as initially thought. Investigate! When Fanny was in a situation that seemed perfect for complaining, she would stare it down. Look it straight in the eye. If you think something is hard, then you have just given life to it, and it will be hard. You can understand the complexity of a situation without giving life to the complaint. Instead, bring life to the solution.

3. Relationships built upon positive energy enjoy a long-lasting life. Through a joyful outlook, leaders are more confident in finding value in others because their self-confidence is not at stake. Positive energy breeds excitement and enthusiasm. People naturally gravitate to others who exude positivity. Fanny cautioned me early in life not to complain about people. "Be positive," she would say. "Build them up. Affirm who they are." She had a unique way of putting things into perspective. "When you complain about others, it is more likely than not what you don't like about yourself."

4. Clarity is gained around situations when you change your perception. You gain a clearer perspective on a situation that you otherwise wouldn't have because you get stuck looking at it from only one point of view. Then the complaining can set in. Can't figure it out? Tired? Take a break. Mom loved working on word search puzzles. The word games with the objective to find the letters that complete the word amongst a random display of other alphabetic letters. When having difficulty finding the line of letters, Fanny would turn her book upside down or on its side and look at the puzzle from different angles. This little twist of perspective allowed her to see the word that was missed. Fanny called it "shaking up the brain."

5. Decision-making is improved when people with a positive nature include others in making choices. Involving others brings more insight, perspective, and knowledge into the process. The saying, "Two heads are better than one," exists for good reason. Including others in the decision-making process, in both life and business, gives you a better chance of finding the best solution the first time.

So how do you stop complaining? Be intentional about how you think and who you choose to be around. Channel your energies towards something that is purposeful, fulfilling, or enlightening. Be cautious that your ego doesn't become too over-inflated, and you fail to recognize even the smallest of blessings. Surround yourself with people who produce a positive impact in and on your life and work, then feed off of that energy.

Be quick to learn who are negative forces in your life, then set some healthy boundaries as to how much time and influence they have on how you think and act. Even though these folks may have good intentions, speaking against life instead of for it will subconsciously bring you down. If you attempt to speak with them, you may not be heard due to their unconscious actions. At this point, it may be time to trim the bush.

Give it a slight trim.

Do some major reshaping.

Cut it down if needed.

It's not about having a positive attitude all the time. It's being genuine and authentic in how you approach life that contributes to the choices you make. Choose the type of people who contribute to you becoming a better person, your best self ever. When you choose to complain, decisions are made based on circumstances. When you take responsibility for your actions, you can focus on solutions.

→ # HOLD THE UMBRELLA

LOOK FOR THE SILVER LINING. Every cloud has one. I make no apologies for looking for a positive outcome, even from the most negative situations. This is what Fanny taught me. She believed it was important to understand that expressing disappointment or being upset was okay. Just don't allow those emotions to control how you think or what you say or do.

There's a familiar analogy about a glass with water in it to the halfway mark. Conventional wisdom suggests that seeing it half full is positive or optimistic and half empty is negative or pessimistic. I suggest that both scenarios can be viewed as positive.

When my glass is half full, I am happy and feeling really good because there is more water to drink. This glass is not empty. Hallelujah. Seeing my glass as half empty gives me an equal amount of delight because there is still water in it to quench my thirst. It's just a matter of perspective and mindset.

To complain or not to complain, that is the question.

Let's face it. We are human and not perfect. We're going to see the negative side of things. It's part of life. Fanny's insight was to minimize complaints, not to eliminate them. She knew that trying to hide complaints or pretend they didn't exist gave them power over you and was limiting in how to respond with character.

Fanny inspired me to temper how I presented my uplifting outlook thinking more of others than myself. Helping others transition from complaint to solution is a unique path for each person. It's important that people have an opportunity to process their emotions and come to terms with the experience before trying to convince them that nobody is listening to their complaint. If I were to project my positive outlook on others, I may miss seeing and understanding the root of their pain in the situation. Helping others through their storms of complaint takes time.

It's not a race.

Be present.

Let it happen.

In the moment, it may not be the right time to offer positive words of encouragement, even if you can see the sunshine beyond the rain or the silver color of your lining. If my friend is standing in the rain letting the drops of water hit her face, getting soaked to the bone, absorbed in the stillness and the circumstances of her life, I see her and want to help. She may not be able to imagine any color in the lining at the moment. What words can I say that will make a difference?

When you don't know what to say, Fanny's counsel was, "Stay quiet and be with them. Stand shoulder to shoulder. Know that their complaint may be coming from a broken place, and although it might be better to snap out of it, that's not what the other person needs right then. There will be plenty of opportunity for snapping. Now isn't the time. Allow the positive moments to emerge. Think about the other person and try to be in their shoes."

In those moments when people are not seeing the positive side of life and find themselves caught in the rain, be the umbrella. Hold a covering over their head to help shelter them from the storm. Let them know they are not alone and be sensitive to how they process through the darkness.

 ## MY LIFE IS A POSTCARD

ON A TRIP TO LISBON, Portugal, I snapped a quick photo of V standing in front of a gift shop on a small street. She was looking at souvenirs to take home to the grandkids. Later that day, I posted the photo on Facebook where a friend liked it and commented that, from his perspective, the photo looked like a postcard.

His comment got me thinking more about perspective and its role in my own life and what Fanny taught me. As I have said before, there is no point in complaining. Every time I begin to go in the direction of thinking negatively about my life, I remember someone I know who has had more challenges. As we commit to changing our perspective on a situation, we open ourselves up to the possibility of new questions, new knowledge, and ultimately better outcomes. Positivity is equally important for a leader. When you are trusted by a team to lead, the impact of a positive attitude cannot be understated.

Keeping a sense of perspective and a positive attitude is ongoing and requires rigorous actions. Our lives and time are precious and need to be treated with the utmost care. Here is some advice Fanny gave me to get that "postcard" treatment in life:

- Understand that circumstances do not determine your happiness or how you respond in this world.
- Choose to think and act with positive energy. When Mom was in pain from Parkinson's and suffering from dementia, we could have had the biggest pity party in town. No one would have stopped us. However, Mom would have kicked my little behind if I had treated her or my own life like it was over. We celebrated every moment together as a blessing.

At an art exhibition in London, I looked at a black and white photo of a small child sitting in rubble on a street. For one moment, it made me sad to look at it until I heard a young woman beside me comment. She suggested that if you looked close enough into the child's eyes, you could see a smile. Imagine if that child, sitting in the rubble with broken glass and cracked buildings all around her, could even hint at a smile, then I could find the strength to see life with a smile as well.

Even when I traveled into third-world countries and saw living conditions worse than anything we'd ever see in the United States, these people were happy. They were grateful for life, welcoming every day with another opportunity to be blessed and thankful for what they had. One of the ladies I met on the street in the market shared that it took as much time to complain as it did to say something nice. She was choosing to focus her energies on making life work.

I am not dismissing the unfortunate hardships of life nor the hatred that exists. I simply choose to celebrate the positive aspects of life. As I have been Fanny-ized, my complaints have been minimized because I fully intend to:

Never apologize for being positive.

Make life work.

Live life like a postcard.

Fanny encouraged us to see the best in life and others. She believed that negative thinking keeps us rooted in the past and does not provide a clear vision of the future. Positivity allows us to move closer to a future where people support each other unconditionally. After Fanny passed away, I read an entry in her journal: "Where there is hope, there is a future."

→ THE BALL AND CHAIN CONUNDRUM

THE PAST REPRESENTS THE SUM of everything we've experienced to this point. When I think of certain times, it's not too difficult to understand why the past has so much power. For some, shedding the past, it's like leaving an old friend behind. And others drag it around wherever they go.

Fanny knew that being trapped in the past could be dangerous and that focusing on our meager beginnings would only determine our meager futures, so she focused her thoughts elsewhere—on more positive outcomes. She often encouraged us with her old adage about the windshield and the rearview mirror. She would speak in a funny voice like she had just inhaled helium from a balloon and say, "The rearview mirror is smaller than the windshield because your future is bigger and more important than your teeny-tiny past." Then we'd laugh. Mom wanted to make sure I knew to put more attention on what was ahead of me versus spending time checking on what was behind me.

Mom also told me I could be anyone I wanted to be. Once I decided then to be the best anyone has ever seen. Although Mom may have shopped second-hand, that did not imply we were less than anyone else. As important as knowing who we were and where we came from, she insisted the past should never overshadow where we were headed.

It's over, essentially dead.

Lifeless, and completely finished.

The future brings new life and hope.

There are "victors" who look forward and understand that the future is what's most important, not what is behind them. These victors realize that getting to a new place requires additional knowledge and that their continued success depends upon a positive mindset, treating others well, and making exceptional character choices. Victors excel at tapping into positive energy and propelling themselves forward; they seek new opportunities with an unlimited spirit and a sense of confidence. Victims, on the other hand, tend to complain that life is not fair; they see others as smarter and given more opportunities. They are often trapped in the past, justifying choices, behavior, and thinking that only inhibits the opportunity for them to learn and grow.

It's important to clarify that the use of the terms "victim" and "victor" in this context are being used in the sense of leadership and not referring to a toxic social situation, understanding the difference between being a victim or a victor depends largely on knowledge, wisdom, and how much time is spent being bound by the past.

Thinking about tomorrow does scare me. There are a lot of unknowns and uncertainty of what's to come. Yet I remain positive and excited about the journey. To be victorious requires setting one's mind to absorb knowledge and being wise enough to know the appropriate actions to use it. The future is not all bright and shiny for everyone. It has victims, too—those who are stuck in their old habits and who cling to how they have always done something.

Comfortable with the status quo.

Afraid of change.

Clinging to what they believe to be right.

If I had clung to that past and bound myself up in it, then traveling the world and having friends in many different countries would have only been a pipe dream. Without these lessons, I would have missed out on earning two post-graduate degrees and authoring a series of books. *Fanny Rules* have transformed into the foundation of my consulting with world leaders and their teams.

It takes rigorous effort and determination to break from the ball and chain to move forward and claim a future unencumbered by outdated traditions, customs, and rituals. My most challenging clients are leaders who see the past as cozy, comfortable, and familiar and the future as scary, uncertain, and uncontrollable. Through a series of consulting techniques, these opportunistic leaders quickly realize that the surest path to future success is to discard the ball and chain that once represented comfort. They must ground themselves and claim victory over one's future by cutting the chains, removing the barriers to a fresh, positive attitude, opening themselves up to learning new ways of thinking, and moving on to a bigger and brighter future.

And do it without complaining, because as Fanny would say, "Ain't nobody listening anyway."

TEACHABLE MOMENTS

- Hold the umbrella—stand in the stillness of the moment and offer comfort and support to someone else without saying a single word. There are times when all someone needs is comfort. They do not need anyone trying to make lemonade out of their lemons or sprinkling fairy dust to ward away the dark clouds of a storm. All they need is silence and to know they are not alone.

- My life is a postcard—explore the wonders of life through the lens of positivity. Applying a positive outlook on life while maintaining standards of being authentic and genuine is no easy feat. Make no apologies for being content and having a healthy, uplifting spirit.

- The ball and chain conundrum—deal with your past and move on. Don't drag it around. Avoid the misfortunate consequences of hanging on to your past for comfort. Acknowledge what has happened in the yesterday of life and move forward. One cannot get to the future if trapped in the past. The only way to the future is through the present. Where there is hope, there is a future.

For your free *Fanny Rules* Teachable Moments Journal go to https://drtroyhall.com/documents/fannyrulesjournal.pdf.

MENTORING LESSONS FOR RULE THREE: POSITIVE MINDSET

Use these questions for a moment of self-reflection and self-discovery:

1. What is your biggest complaint in life, and why?
2. Identify at least three solutions for the problem after you stop complaining and offer yourself as a solution.
3. Think about the last time you complained about something and after some time realized it wasn't really that important.
4. What qualities and characteristics would you change?
5. What would you keep to live your life as a postcard?
6. Complete this sentence: I will no longer settle for being a victim held by my past. Instead I claim a future of ___

_____.

FANNY DIDN'T RAISE NO FOOL

"Character is defined by choices, not circumstances."

MOM TAUGHT ME THAT PEOPLE ALWAYS HAVE OPTIONS.

IT'S A MATTER OF WHO you are going to be in the situation. And the choices you make are the decisions you live by. It sounds easy and straightforward, yet it can be complicated when circumstances are given a higher priority than character. Mom would suggest that you make choices as though they will show up somewhere on the outside of your body, not hidden inside where they are easily concealed. Wear your choices proudly. "If you are a reflection of your choices," she would proclaim, "what would you look like in the mirror? How do you want others to see you?"

Making decisions without ever considering the consequences to others is what Mom would have called ego-pride. This is when you desire the attention and want others to look upon you in God-like fashion. You act for the benefit of self, not in consideration of others. With ego-pride, a dark shadow is cast, and negative consequences are sure to follow. We slide into a selfish place and forget that the actions we are taking or going to make could indirectly harm the ones we love the most. Those consequences are a by-product of pushing a personal agenda or ruling with authoritative power. The rush of being in charge begins to overtake why the leader is actually leading in the first place.

On more than one occasion, Fanny reminded me, "Character is defined by choices, not circumstances." In her teachings, character-choices involve the decisions one makes based on the attributes of being teachable, showing compassion, extending grace, seeking truth, displaying humility, acting with pure intentions, and offering peace. These seven attributes of effective leadership are the foundation of making decisions based upon choices that consider outcomes that benefit both you and others.

Circumstances are simply the things that happen in our daily lives. They are events—occurrences of man or nature that seem to occur at the most inopportune times. Circumstances are the details surrounding a situation or a condition that causes something to happen. If not put into proper perspective, people will blame circumstances for how they think, speak to others, and behave. Circumstances don't define a person. They are situations and experiences that happen in a person's immediate surroundings. It's the choices that determine the value of success or failure, not the events of the day.

A classic example illustrating the difference between character choice and circumstantial influence involves two students, each receiving an "A" on a test. One student explains the "A" as the material being easy to understand and that the teacher likes them, too. The other student owns the "A" and realizes the work they put into getting that grade—studying hard, paying attention in class, and completing all the homework assignments leading up to the test. The first student explained the grade based on circumstantial influence, having no control over the outcome. The second student took ownership of their choices to study, pay attention, and complete the required assignments.

One of my earliest recollections of understanding the power of defining my character by choice over circumstances came when the kids teased one of my best friends. She and I had known each other since we were three years old. We played hide-n-seek at my house, shared peanut butter sandwiches, and drank Kool-Aid. In fact, she was also the first girl I had ever kissed. One of my very special treats was going to her home for dinner. Her mama sure knew how to put out a spread of food. My favorite meal was the fish fry on Christmas Eve. The fried fish was dipped in homemade sauce, and the warm double chocolate chip fudge brownies were topped with a dollop of whipped cream and a cherry.

One day, while playing at school during recess, a group of "cool kids" began to make what seemed like at the time funny comments about my friend's name, how she looked and acted. As the other kids hurled insults, I chose to laugh with them. I failed to make a positive character choice and support my friend for who she was, not what others saw as her weaknesses. On that day, my decision-making abilities were not at their best.

Inconsiderate.

Guilty.

Ashamed.

There are no secrets when living in a small town. It didn't take Mom long to figure out what had happened. She was very upset and stood there without blinking, giving me "the eye." You know the one—the stink eye. There was no escaping her gaze. At first, I was all about blaming the other kids for the words. "Hey, they started it. I didn't say anything. I only laughed." Mom was not amused, nor was she going to tolerate that excuse or any concoction of a story I made up to justify my horrible behavior. There was no squirming or trying to weasel out of it. That day, I had chosen to be one of the "cool kids" and not a best friend. My choice did not define my character in a good way. I allowed the circumstances of the kids' actions to justify my behavior.

Boy, did I get a lecture that evening. "If you fail to stand for something, you may never stand for anything at all." Fanny expected me to stand beside my friend, not behind her. Mom even added a little extra persuasion to make her point. When I was growing up, Parenting 101 included the concept, "If you spare the rod, you spoil the child." On this day, Fanny was not in the sparing mood, and I truly got a *fanny*-lecture.

Man, how I hate it when I let others down. On that day, I discovered that when you let someone down, especially someone who has counted on you, it's worse than letting yourself down. I was so disappointed in my performance that day. It was a defining moment for sure, and I knew the only way to make it right was to express my sorrow to my friend and ask for her forgiveness. Although she quickly forgave me, it took quite a while before I forgave myself.

When individuals make character choices based on their moral beliefs, they demonstrate a high level of control. People of character make decisions on how strongly they believe in and about their convictions, not the events of the day or others' actions. Allowing circumstances to influence decision-making signifies that a person believes more in what is happening in their environment that surrounds them than they believe in themselves being in control of these events.

Successful leaders make character choices a regular part of their decision-making process. They are aware of circumstances and all the dynamics these events assert in their lives. Leaders who possess strong character understand that choosing to do the right thing is not always the easiest. Every choice considers friends, family, colleagues, and even strangers. This type of leader also doesn't waver on their decision to do what's right based on positive moral and ethical convictions and beliefs. It takes a strong will and determination to make character choices even if it means taking a stand for a friend or someone in trouble in the face of personal ridicule, political injustice, or social shaming.

HE WHO HAS THE CLICKER
IS IN CONTROL

WHEN IT COMES TO OUR WORK, there's a certain level of control that every professional wants to have when it comes time to present their idea to the world. In one instance, I had carefully planned out every detail for a talk I was giving in an auditorium-style venue. I worked it out with the crew to ensure I was standing in the right position, keeping in mind where the cameras were located. We checked the camera angles, too, tested the microphone, fussed with the podium, and advanced the first two slides in my presentation to make sure the clicker was working.

After returning from my dressing area wearing a blazer, khakis, and collared shirt, I stopped by to see the technicians to thank them for the preparation. Tim, the technician assigned to me that day, saw me looking inside my blazer pockets, around the counter, in my pockets again, glancing up toward the stage, back into the pockets for one more look. He interrupted my unproductive routine and asked, "What did you lose?" Still searching the same places I had already looked, without making eye contact, I responded, "The clicker."

Tim gave a quick little chuckle, which turned into a serious face when we did make eye contact. He saw that I was not kidding. Sheepishly, he said, "You don't have a clicker." My internal voice was screaming, "What? No clicker? Come on, Timmy, oh boy, oh pal, you're kidding me, right?"

It was almost showtime, and I tried my best to act like I was okay with this horrible joke. But alas, it wasn't a joke. There wasn't a clicker to advance the presentation. I discovered later that presenters at this venue typically used a script, so the technicians would simply follow along and advance their presentation based on keywords within the text and slides. Being an extemporaneous speaker, I use keywords on the slide combined with the reaction of the audience to shape my message and its delivery.

So, I asked Tim, "How will I advance the slides?"

"Oh, we'll do that for you," Tim said.

In a few split seconds, I had to make a choice. Was I going to express my disappointment by raising my voice, asserting my stature as a paid speaker, and wallow in my circumstances, or would I take the high road, show character, and go with the flow?

Fortunately, Fanny's words about choice echoed in my head, much like how a muscle responds after it has practiced a particular movement over and over again. The choice was clear, and my decision was made: I had to choose character over circumstance.

With Tim's help, we devised a cueing system to use that would signal each time he needed to advance a slide. On stage, I had a faux clicker, and each time I pointed it toward the giant screens on stage, my buddy, Tim, would take it from there. Within minutes, we created an innovative solution to help me have "control" even though I was "clickerless" for the next hour. In this case, the circumstance did not rule the choice. My problem was solved, and just as my introductory video had finished and I was about to step on stage, Tim added one more caveat: "Uh, the animation in your presentation won't be visible, either." Again, I screamed inside my head. Then I laughed it off. This was a test, a test I planned to pass. A test to show the type of leader Fanny had taught me to be. I went up on stage and delivered a knockout presentation.

No clicker.

No animation.

No problem.

In the end, the audience would've had no idea if this teachable moment actually occurred moments prior to the start of the presentation or if I just worked it in, but the story fit because I wanted the leaders in that room to have a clear example of choice over circumstances. Not so they would be proud of me, but to help them become proud of themselves each time they chose character. Character defines the person. Fanny taught me, "No one can take your character away from you, but if you're careless, you just might give it away."

That wasn't for me. Not this day.

PRIORITY OR POPULARITY

EVERYONE WANTS TO BE POPULAR, RIGHT? But the popular choice is not necessarily the one with the highest level of priority, and popular decisions do not always lead to the greatest reward. Choosing popularity over priority may be the easiest because it generally involves the path of least resistance. However, the responsibility of the leader is to make good choices, not easy ones.

Popularity can come in different forms other than just about being liked. Sometimes we make popular choices because others have made it an acceptable option. For example, fashionable clothing and material possessions deemed to be in high demand, almost de facto to a form of being popular as they, too, reflect the most common choice.

When you grow up in a family with modest means, you count every penny, nickel, and dime you earn, and if you're lucky, you get to count some of the coins twice for good measure. Being budget-conscious, Fanny taught us to shop with a frugal mindset. Mom was a master at making two nickels into a quarter, and she always looked for the best deals.

One afternoon, Mom and my niece went shopping for school clothes. It was more than a thirty-minute drive from our little town to a grocery or department store, so there was plenty of time for girl talk on the way into the city. Naturally, the conversation turned to fashion—the colors, the look, and the feel. As they drove toward the city, country music played on the radio, the hillbilly air conditioning at full force—windows open—and the car swerving to miss potholes. It was almost as fun as riding a roller coaster when Fanny was behind the wheel.

My niece, the daughter of my sister who is nine years my senior, had her heart set on one particular school outfit. She had cut out pictures from the Sears and Roebuck catalog and taped them to a piece of paper so they would be top of mind. When the car stopped in the city, my niece quickly realized where they were. Her eyes got as big as the saucers on Aunt Millie's favorite tea set. Holding back the tears, she got out of the car and carefully closed the door. Mom and my niece stood in front of the local thrift shop, not the fancy department store.

Disappointed.

Upset.

Heartbroken.

Mom put an arm around her and gave her a tender kiss on the head and offered a sweet smile of reassurance to say, "We've got this." With her purse on one arm and the hand of her granddaughter on the other, they entered the store. Mom reached into her pocket and took out a carefully folded piece of paper. It was my niece's fashion collage. In a shocked voice, still being respectful, my niece asked, "Why did you bring that piece of paper? We're not going to find those clothes here."

"That's right," Fanny replied, and with a wink, she added, "We're going to find something better." Now whether or not my niece believed it, Fanny did, and when Fanny believed it, the rest of us got religion, too.

It took several hours of carefully mixing and matching, trying on, and putting back. Finally, Mom scored and found several pieces of clothing that would do just fine. She knew how to fix them up, dust them off, and make them look like new. My niece didn't get what she had her heart set on—she got the ones that were the best buy for the money they had. In this mentoring lesson, Fanny taught her that you could be just as successful shopping with a priority mindset as when you buy with popularity.

This little trip and its outcome were the norms for our family, not the exceptions. Mom had this knack for taking the most out-of-date, downtrodden item and giving it new life. When it was time for her to shop for my brother and me, Mom often took us to this low-budget department store called Hills. We thought it was a big deal mostly because we got to ride the penny pony out front if we had been good inside.

Each year, I proudly wore fashionable Hills clothing on my first day of school. Mom said they came from the best designer rack in the store. It wasn't until I got to high school that I realized "CLEARANCE" wasn't a brand name.

When prioritizing, it's essential to avoid decisions that simply please other people. Leaders must be able to separate refusal from rejection, realizing you cannot please everyone all the time. Consider the Return on Time (ROT) and Return on Investment (ROI) as part of the economic decision-making factors. Sometimes decisions involve resource allocation and setting minimums of time and resources to maximize effort and effectiveness for winning results.

Prioritizing actions that produce desired results—those that are meaningful and intentional—means the leader will contemplate all angles leading to the goal. These leaders will consider being open-minded and listening to the voice of their most trusted council. Finally, leaders who understand prioritization integrate both self and others' feelings and know that the final choice is always within the leader's purview. The very best decision may very well be the choice of priority and popularity. It's rare when the stars align in this fashion, but it can happen.

Fanny had a unique way of summing up popularity: "Someone who makes choices to be liked doesn't require much information." She was right. Choosing not to take the road most traveled, the fashion that is trending, or acquiescing to the need to be liked takes knowledge, a discerning spirit, and a fair amount of guts to make the right call.

THE BLUE ROOF PRINCIPLE:
PEOPLE OVER PROFIT

DECISIONS, DECISIONS, DECISIONS.

We make thousands of decisions every single day, yet most people hate making them. Lack of clarity and fear plays a significant role in indecision, leading to procrastination and anxiety. Decisions mean taking action, and taking action means consequences, both positive and negative—a terrifying thought to most. Yet the ability to be decisive is one of the critical roles of effective leadership.

"Anyone can make the easy decisions," Fanny said. "It's the hard ones that build character."

Leaders are often caught in a conundrum. They must decide what to do for the good of an entire team. Sometimes the choices are easy; sometimes they are not. So how do we make the tough choices, the choices whose consequences will impact multiple people or entire organizations?

When I have to make critical decisions in my organization, I apply what I call *The Blue Roof Principle*. Most lessons we learn and apply in business generally start from personal experience, and The Blue Roof Principle is no exception. As part of the teachings of The Blue Roof Principle, the question posed is, "At what cost would you push forward to get your way?" In other words, you either fight for people or profit.

Meet two future retirees who had dreamed for nearly forty years on how their forever home would look. They planned every aspect of the house, even down to their guest's experience from the moment they drove up, the parking of the car, the entry walkway, and the greeting at the oversized double front doors. It was sure to be magnificent.

These two individuals knew that building their dream home would present challenges along the way. They were building in a unique neighborhood with rigorous adherence to building codes and materials. Knowing this, they created a plan to include every detail of their dream home, from fixtures to furniture, flooring to wall coverings. This also included a repeating color theme for this dream home. (Spoiler alert: that color was blue.)

Knowing the requirements and wanting to abide by the rules, the soon-to-be retirees worked with their builder to make sure everything was approval-ready before construction began. After months of review and consideration, the homeowner's association approved the entire plan, including outdoor paint, hardscape materials, roofing, window placement, and driveway access. Their dream home was about to come to life.

What they didn't realize was they were about to face "The Blue Roof Principle."

One bright, sunny afternoon, they received a call from the builder with some disappointing news. After the roof was nearly fifty percent installed, the homeowner's association decided the individual who approved it had made a mistake. A blue roof did not fit the neighborhood's overall concept and design.

You've got to be kidding.

We have approval.

Can they do this?

From a pragmatic perspective, it just didn't seem right. All the approvals had been garnered months in advance, along with samples of the exterior color scheme that were prominently displayed on the job site for quick and easy reference by the builders. It was hard for this soon-to-be-retired couple to understand precisely how this shift in approval could have happened.

What was the cost of getting the blue roof? There were many varying layers of consideration taken into account. For the most part, these potential owners of their dream home did not want to start life in a forever haven that would be the center of attention and controversy. Would there be hidden consequences for the individual who approved the roof color? Would the governing body lose trust in the builder if they went forward with the blue roof?

Now, they had to choose how to move forward.

What would be the choice, and at what cost?

They considered this impasse an opportunity to be an act of leadership. It was important to weigh the potential negative consequences that could impact everyone involved. Finally, they made up their minds. Although the blue roof started as a fantastic addition to the home, it wasn't worth the fight in the end.

Did they have the energy for a fight?

Were resources available to sustain a fight?

What was the cost of a fight?

The energy and resources were not issues; neither was their ability to follow through. However, after careful consideration of the potential damage to the others involved, the cost would be too high to continue the battle over the blue roof. In the end, they chose the people involved in the situation and not the roof. They chose character over circumstance.

Winning the blue roof was not the right fight. Instead, they made a leadership choice that placed others' interests above their own: people over profit. It wasn't the easiest decision, yet it was the right one.

These future homeowners chose to stand for the needs and concerns of others first, ahead of their own. They settled for their second choice in roof color and let life move on. In five, ten, or twenty years, who would know anyway? The people whose lives were touched by an act of character would always remember, however. It was a big win in the long run because putting people over profit will always be the winning choice.

TEACHABLE MOMENTS

- He who has the clicker is in control—not everything works out as planned. How one deals with adversity, in even the most controlled situations, will be a defining moment. The choices are simple—character or circumstance. Choose wisely.

- Priority or popularity—sometimes you have to choose between the important or safe option. Do what is right or do what is more readily accepted. Never lose sight of the fact you have free will, and if you believe in luck, then maybe your final decision will include a little of both.

- The Blue Roof Principle: people over profit—choosing relationships over financial rewards come at a cost. Making the right decision is not always the easy choice. Oftentimes, it takes will and determination to do what is right for the many and not the one.

For your free *Fanny Rules* Teachable Moments Journal go to https://drtroyhall.com/documents/fannyrulesjournal.pdf.

MENTORING LESSONS FOR RULE FOUR: CHOICES OVER CIRCUMSTANCES

When considering whether to choose character over circumstance, think about:

1. What do you look like in the mirror after making a difficult choice?
2. How would others interpret the image you are casting about that choice?
3. Is there a difference between what you and others see?
4. Who is your accountability partner?
5. What is your definition of integrity?
    *   Does it include doing the right thing whether anyone is watching or not?
    *   Are your choices supported with good moral, ethical, and legal behaviors?
6. Who will you stand up for today?

SINK, SWIM, OR JUST TREAD WATER

"Sinking was never an option."

DON'T BE AN ACCIDENTAL LEADER. BE ONE OF PURPOSE AND STRENGTH.

MOM WAS THE TYPE of woman who looked for the good in me and in others, always reminding us what we did well. If I could learn to identify and bring meaning to my strengths, I would have the ability to help others develop their strengths, too. Fanny always said that focusing on one's strengths allows us to see the very best in others and ourselves and that affirming people—giving them credit for who they are and who they would become in the future—is essential in developing their confidence and determination to succeed. This sweet lady had a God-given knack for building great relationships with young, old, rich or poor, black or white. And more times than not, she was good at it.

Really.

Really.

Good at it.

Mom had an unbelievable ability to relate to people. With a high degree of emotional intelligence, Fanny stressed the importance of building solid relations. She did this largely by managing how she processed others' feelings and emotions and responded to them. She was a master at this because she had a keen understanding of how people might feel in any situation.

Mom didn't know the fancy terms like diversity, equity, inclusion, or emotional intelligence. What she knew, however, was how to treat people right regardless of demographics or stature. She knew how to listen, understand, and empathize, rarely putting herself ahead of another. This did not mean she was perfect at relationships. Fanny said there were times when she had to eat a piece of humble pie. But those times were rare.

Fanny would also remind me that relationships could get messy from time to time. It would be hard work because people do try one's patience at times. They don't always respond exactly how you'd like them to or even how you think they will. However, if you persist and stay the course, in the end, it will be worth it. Mom encouraged me to learn as much as I could and to put that knowledge into action. Fanny told me that learning would be my strength, but it would become a weakness if I failed to put that knowledge into action. "Knowledge is power. Wisdom is more powerful because you have put what you learned into action."

Mom thought it was good to know a little about a lot of things but warned against skimming on important topics. If I were to dabble in learning many things, then I would have a broad scope of knowledge yet not have a concentration in anything. She encouraged me to find something I liked or wanted to do and go deeper into the subject matter. I enjoyed helping others and teaching. Seeing the joy in others' faces when I was able to contribute and help them out made my day. Some of my desire for mentoring came from wanting to share what I had learned. This was my way of putting that knowledge into action. Fanny said I was born to lead and teach. Little did I know—until later in life—how important it was to become an expert on a particular topic.

Much time has passed since Fanny first introduced this lesson, the undertone of which eventually contributed to my pursuit of graduate work. When I began my formal career, working with people helped me build my strength and knowledge in leadership—gradually building my confidence as a leader. As my experience grew, I transitioned into the specific area of talent retention. Sadly, Mom's fight with dementia toward the end of her life kept her from fully realizing the fruits of her labor. Fanny's little boy earned a PhD in Global Leadership & Entrepreneurship.

Today, I consult with leaders on the topics of culture and leadership, strategy, and change. Through my keynote addresses and workshops, I speak to audiences around the world about the benefits of retaining talent by building culture of cohesion where people feel a sense of belonging, are valued and share in mutual commitments. I know Mom would have been so proud.

REMEMBER THE DENT

MY BROTHER-IN-LAW, RON, is five years younger than me. He recounted his earliest memory of Mom. At the time, V and I were in high school and had just started dating. Ron remembered coming over to our house one summer afternoon to hang out with my brother. Dad had worked for weeks repairing two old minibikes for us to ride around the property. He welded the hot-red frames to make sure they were sturdy and could take the dips, turns, and slope of the hillside. Dad even rebuilt the engines from spare parts of several old lawnmowers. They were so much fun to ride!

My brother-in-law's story went like this:

"Troy's brother and I decided to race each other up and down the hill on minibikes. After a quick lesson, we were off. To save face, I did not disclose that I had never ridden a vehicle with an engine. Literally, I had no idea of the power and the precision needed to safely guide this homemade all-terrain vehicle. Like most first-time lessons associated with learning how to ride a traditional bike, we spent a lot of my training on how to use the throttle and clutch. Before I had a chance to figure out how to stop this crazy thing, I heard these three words.

Ready.

Set.

Go.

I looked toward the hill, gunned the engine, released the clutch, and took off. Troy's brother shot off first straight for the target. My demon-possessed minibike had a mind of its own.

Within seconds, I was headed toward the side of the house, not the hill. My reflexes kicked into gear, but it was too late.

CRASH.

BANG.

BOOM.

The foot-pedal of the minibike hit the corner of the house, denting the siding. I found myself lying flat, face down on the ground. Thankfully, the minibike had fallen away from me. Of course, Troy's brother thought this was the coolest thing he had ever seen. He laughed so hard. I would have joined him if my pride had not just been crushed.

Troy's mom came running out of the house, asking if I was okay. There was this nauseous feeling coming over me as she drew closer. I confessed what happened and how sorry I was. She hugged me, told me not to give it another thought, and suggested I could use some more training in the open field away from the house. She had a way about her that made me feel like I was another one of her kids. His mom showed me compassion and a Christ-like grace that let me know I was forgiven. She also refused to allow me to pay for any repairs.

As an adult, I learned Fanny decided not to fix the dent in the siding. She said it reminded her of that little boy. If she only knew today how thinking of that dent makes me think of her. Fanny was one of the kindest people I have ever had the *honor* of knowing."

Mom helped the young boy, who had no ill-intent of destroying property, find courage, confidence, and determination to get back up and ride again. Fanny used that opportunity to remind my brother-in-law of his strength and not belittle him because of his weakness. That's how it is when leaders focus on strengths and not flaws. Our strengths, not the weaknesses, help us drive toward achieving our goals. Mentoring at its finest.

→ EXPEND ENERGY ON YOUR STRENGTHS

FOR EVERY STRENGTH, there is a weakness, and each vulnerability has a counter-balanced strength. Often, we make a list of each and treat the two as mutually exclusive when, in fact, strengths and weaknesses have a "yin-yang" kind of relationship. This concept of dualism is part of ancient Chinese philosophy. What may appear at first blush to be seemingly opposite forces, these two relatable sets of values exhibit a complementary and connected relationship to one another.

Successful leaders of transformation understand this relational concept between strengths and weaknesses. One effective coaching exercise I use is to have a leader identify one of their strengths. They describe it and give context to why it is a strength and has value. Then I ask, "How can your strength become a weakness?" This thought process uncovers the nuances of both the strengths and weaknesses that may have gone unnoticed. Understanding how strength can slip into weakness provides the leader with access to knowledge that impacts behavior. Then it's up to the leader to put this information into action.

The same process can be used to further examine a weakness. My inquiry is, "What strength do you have that can offset this particular weakness?" We make a note of the response and use it to drive toward success. It's not just identifying strengths and weaknesses that make the exercise work. When the leader has access to this valuable information that lies beneath the surface, they now have power. They have even more power when this newfound knowledge is put into action.

When we focus on our strengths, we have an opportunity to move forward. Our strengths help us to improve, to achieve. Our weaknesses can hold us back or keep us stuck in one place. I think of my strengths and weaknesses as relating to the metaphor of sinking, swimming, or treading water. Swimming is working my strengths while treading water is improving a weakness, and sinking, well, you've given up.

Imagine you find yourself in the center of a deep body of water, at least deep enough where you can't see or touch the bottom. You look all around and finally catch a glimpse of land off in the distance. In this scenario, your mind settles on one of three options.

Sink.

Swim.

Tread water.

If you did nothing, the outcome would be to sink, but that's not how you want the story to end. Instead, you pull yourself together and remember how adept you are at moving your arms and legs. You try a circular motion with your arms while moving your legs like you're riding an imaginary bike in the water. This technique will help you keep your head above water. However, you remain stationary. Think of this type of movement as if you are working on a weakness. You may even get good at it. Still, you're not moving forward. Instead, you become really good at staying in one place.

The other option is for you to move your arms and legs into a motion that propels your body forward. You put your head into the water and burst forward as you move your arms and legs. Instead of circular motions with your arms, you propel your arms forward, one after the other, extending them into the water over your head. Your hands pull back toward you, scooping the water. Now, your legs and feet are kicking as if you are taking a brisk walk. You're working your arms and legs to propel you forward, moving you closer to your goal. This type of action is like focusing on one of your strengths. You improve and fine-tune your strength with each stroke.

Any one of us can expend an equal amount of energy moving our arms and legs, but without the forward motion, we're still just treading water. When the attention is on a weakness, we may see some improvement. But it's not necessarily going to produce a result of moving toward our goals. However, when we focus on strengths, we move forward.

Metaphorically speaking, I prefer to swim. Besides, as far as Fanny was concerned, sinking was never an option.

→ CONFIDENCE AND DETERMINATION BUILD STRENGTHS

MOM AND DAD LOVED CAMPING. When we were growing up, they would regularly share their escapades with us. When they were first married, on Friday nights, they'd head to their favorite spot alongside a stream. Their "tent" was their 1940s Mercury station wagon, where they'd fold down the back seats and roll out a foam mattress and place sleeping bags on top. Early morning breakfast was served just after the sun rose. Mom would open the car's tailgate and out would come the Coleman stove. While Dad was off catching their lunch and dinner in the nearby stream, Mom would fire up the single burner to perk that dark, magic brew. Every morning started with a steaming pot of hot Maxwell House Coffee. They loved a good cup of coffee, even to the last drop. Mom always had a cup waiting for him when he returned with their bounty.

They knew their strengths and played well with them. Dad was the protector and provider. Mom was the nurturer and caregiver. These were not just roles; they embodied their strengths and never begrudged the other for what they did or how they went about doing it. Mom and Dad were a team.

Over the years, the camping got a little more sophisticated. Their excursion experiences evolved with each new form of housing. What began as a station wagon for shelter was then upgraded to a canvas tent, then to Dad's homemade version of a tear-drop trailer, to the bread truck he converted into a moving camper ending with a professionally constructed motorhome, which even had a hitch on the back to haul the small motor-powered fishing boat.

Dad did most of the driving in those days, but Mom could hold her own. She was the one who had the skill for backing the trailers and motorhomes with perfect precision into their spots. She did it while watching him through the side-view mirror. Those two knew how to support each other's strengths and build a family and a life full of memories through sixty-five years of marriage.

As time went by, modern conveniences allowed Mom to make the coffee, put it in a Thermos, and join Dad with early morning fishing on their boat. With Dad's experience, he taught Mom to fish, and she took it all in with ease. Mom was a quick learner, and that little lady held her own against the best of them! She even learned how to drive the boat and fish.

One day upon returning from a successful fishing expedition, they approached the riverbank in their small fishing boat, where several of Dad's friends talked near the boat ramp.

They made eye contact with Mom.

She saw them, too.

Fanny looked at Slim.

He looked back at her with a level of uncertainty about what should happen next. Mom had only learned how to drive the boat a few weeks prior. This was supposed to be another simple practice run. Dad was the expert when it came to maneuvering the boat into the slip and onto the ramp. She had watched him often, but we all know that watching is not the same thing as doing. People who have mastered a skill make it look effortless; therefore, others can often approach the same act with overconfidence, thinking it may be easy.

Dad looked over and said, "Mommy, I know you can do this. Just remember what I taught you. But if you want, I can take it from here." She knew the men were his friends, and if this didn't go well...well, you get the picture. They were watching and waiting. Fanny replied confidently, "Nope, I got this."

Before anyone knew what was happening, Fanny turned her ball cap around, so the bill was facing away from the back of her head. She gunned the engine and, with a flip of the wheel, perfectly turned the boat one hundred eighty degrees and slid it sideways into its spot. It was like perfect, parallel parking on the water. They then traded places, so Dad could finish bringing it up the ramp for loading. Mom got out of the boat and, in typical Fanny style, moved her cap back around, nodded to the men, and kept walking toward the pickup.

Dad enjoyed telling the story of Fanny and the motorboat. I think he got a big kick out of seeing the jaw-dropping look on their faces as the petite little lady strolled past them with all the confidence and assurance of a job well done. During one of our campfire chats, I asked her how she did it.

Mom took a sip of her coffee.

Leaned back in her chair.

Put her feet up on the ledge of the fire pit.

Then very calmly said, "For the life of me, all I remember is this: I saw those men who didn't think a woman could handle a boat. It just fired up something inside of me. So, I turned my ball cap around, asked God, 'Please don't let me make a fool of myself in front of Slim's friends.' Then I closed my eyes and gunned the engine. The rest is history."

Dad's confidence in Mom may have given her the strength to pull off the motorboat victory. It could have been beginner's luck. Whatever it was, Fanny took a risk and defined her character. The circumstantial facts of limited experience and a group of gawking men would not deny this extraordinary woman the opportunity to put what she had learned into action.

LESSONS FROM *GILLIGAN'S ISLAND*

IT WAS MEANT TO BE a three-hour tour.

Aside from playing Batman & Robin with my imaginary friends and hide-n-seek with my real friends, growing up in a small town offered limited forms of entertainment. We weren't wholly uncivilized. The town enjoyed annual events such as the church ice cream social, craft bazaar, and the annual fire department carnival. That's where I first learned to play ring toss and gained the courage to ride the Spider, a highly sought-after, eight-legged carnival ride. The Spider was known for being able to spin dry your dunking-tank-drenched shirt in seconds and, if not careful, bring forth a liquid version of two hot dogs smothered in mustard and onions, side of fries with ketchup, and funnel cake covered in powdered sugar.

Of course, when not lured to these big-top events and after a long day playing outside, we were allowed to watch one or two TV shows before going to bed. My favorite, which became a Saturday night tradition for several years, was watching the sitcom *Gilligan's Island*. I could hardly wait to see what was in store for Gilligan, the Skipper, the Millionaire and his Wife, the Movie Star, the Professor, and Mary Anne.

After taking our "weekly baths," we would get out the playing cards and watch TV. My brother was three years younger than me and off to bed earlier, so Mom and I would play Canasta, enjoy the taffy candy called Sugar Daddy, and watch the castaways try to find their way home.

The story of the shipwrecked SS *Minnow* began as a three-hour tour until it ended up in a storm at sea and crashed on a deserted isle. For the most part, the story was about a group of quirky characters and their ill-achieved rescue attempts. To ensure survival and the hope of going home, the seven castaways worked together using all of their combined strengths.

Sometimes that's how it is in life. We find ourselves in a group of people we barely know and are thrust into a process of working toward a common goal. Like with the stranded castaways, our experiences with our company-like island require us to use our combined individual strengths to find success. What was most interesting to me was how each episode found a unique way to showcase one or more strengths of the castaways. No matter which character was featured as the lead, somehow, all of the castaways were involved in solving the weekly dilemma. And no matter how hard they tried, their crazy antics resolved the situations. Each person had unique value, and when they combined forces, it ignited a synergy that most companies would want to bottle and pour out when needed. If we move past the fact the show was a comedy—and being rescued in the first episode would have stunted the show's three-season run—some really great moments highlighted their individual and collective strengths.

Gilligan was a little quirky, to say the least. He often did most of the heavy lifting around the island and rarely complained. He had a good personality and was well-liked by the Skipper and his fellow island mates. However, when he had the opportunity to lead, he was notorious for making the most obscure and outlandish suggestions.

He had an idea.

The castaways laughed.

Then the spark.

The Professor had the knack for taking those insane suggestions and reinventing them into workable solutions to solve the storyline's needs. Of course, this was a comedy, so the concept of these real people with real strengths was absurd. Yet Mom could turn the weekly sitcom into a teachable moment when the opportunity arose.

In addition to Gilligan and Skipper's bumbling antics, it was fascinating how they could create many useful objects from supplies found on the island, such as bamboo, vines, and abandoned artifacts. They made cooking utensils and framed huts from bamboo with thatched roofs and walls made of grass. During one episode, the

Professor created a lie-detector apparatus using spare parts from their ship-wrecked boat. These fantasy-made inventions inspired my childhood creativity and fueled my desire to make things with leftover objects found around the house.

Mom helped me realize that in order to develop my strengths, I needed to focus on them. "Work them like a muscle so they will get stronger," she would say. "And consistently developing your strengths will enable you to grow and help others to develop." This lesson led me to adopt a growth mindset of moving forward and not remaining stuck in one place. Basically, never giving up!

Fanny mentored me in a way to focus on developing my brain power and think about what was required to satisfy any situation, problem, or concern. She encouraged me to apply my strengths of imagination and creativity.

Make crafts.

Solve puzzles.

Be creative and innovative.

Look for what is around and see how it could be used. Put different combinations of things together to make something original. Don't limit yourself to what you already have comprehended or experienced. Seek new wisdom, obtain input from others, and make sure that my creative spirit solves the need, not just a desire to create.

Hold onto your hat Skipper, Innovation and Creativity are the subjects for Rule 6.

TEACHABLE MOMENTS

- Remember the dent—symbolism is a powerful tool to express a belief in your future abilities. Oftentimes some quirky image reminds us of something or someone special. It is a token memory and brings forth an impactful experience that allows you to relive the event in your mind. When the event is positive, it helps you build confidence, a powerful strength.

- Expend energy on your strengths—use your talents, resources, and energy to propel yourself forward to attain your goals. If you can expend an equal amount of effort to achieve something positive as you would to stand still, or worse yet attain a negative outcome, then where do you want to spend your time? Focus on your strengths. Every time you develop your strength, your weaknesses naturally get better. But if you only focus on your weaknesses, then your strength remains stagnant.

- Confidence and determination build strengths—sometimes confidence is sparked by a belief someone else has in you. The teachable moment ties in very nicely with the "Remember the Dent."

- Lessons from *Gilligan's Island*—focus on one another's strengths to build a cohesive team. Not everyone is alike, and that is a good thing. A healthy and highly functioning team focuses on individual positive contributions that contribute to the collective body of work that attains a common objective.

For your free *Fanny Rules* Teachable Moments Journal go to https://drtroyhall.com/documents/fannyrulesjournal.pdf.

MENTORING LESSONS FOR RULE FIVE: BUILD YOUR STRENGTHS

Strengths Self-Assessment Worksheet

Instructions: Complete the following self-assessment sheet to rank the individual categories of leadership strength. Read the information associated with each strength and choose the number that best describes your confidence in that area. You may circle it or place an "X" over the number. The rating scale for this assessment is: 10–9 consistent, 8–7 most of the time, 6–4 not often enough, and 3–1 need help.

SOCIAL ARCHITECT

1   2   3   4   5   6   7   8   9   10

You are good with people, know how to build trust. You modify your leadership style to adapt to others. As a social architect, you have deep relationships with people in both your personal and professional realms.

To score 9 or 10, you regularly are asked to share your perspective or offer advice. People see you as a leader who puts others first.

For a score of 6 or below, you have been told on more than one occasion that you are abrupt or abrasive with others. You often lose your patience when asked to repeat instructions or information. Others feel you cannot keep information confidential. You try to be the life of the party even when there is already plenty of life.

Do not rate yourself based on being an intro- or extrovert. This is about the quality of your relationships with people in your personal and professional life, not your level of outgoingness.

INTERCULTURAL SENSITIVITY
1 2 3 4 5 6 7 8 9 10

Your mind is open to the knowledge, awareness and acceptance of other cultures. You seek to learn more about people who think, act, and look different than you do. You understand acceptance is not agreement.

To score 9 or 10, you must regularly encourage interactions and show support and adoption of diversity, equity, and inclusion practices and principles.

To score a 6 or below, you are guilty of making remarks that single out an individual for gender, race, disability, sexual orientation, or age. You believe your views about culture are the best and cannot understand why others do not think as you do.

COMMUNICATION
1 2 3 4 5 6 7 8 9 10

You are actively involved in the transfer and exchange of knowledge and feelings with others in an upward, downward, and/or sideways direction. You keep people in the loop, letting them know what is happening that impacts their work or home life as appropriate.

To score 9 or 10, you have been affirmed by others that you listen, show compassion, and have demonstrated empathy toward another person.

For a score of 6 or below, you tend to keep people in the dark. Those around you are often surprised to learn important information that could help them complete their tasks. You tend to shy away from calling, emailing, or texting because you don't have time or don't see value in a lot of communication.

SELF-REGARD

1   2   3   4   5   6   7   8   9   10

As a leader, you exhibit a self-regulating behavior to be conscientious of your relations with others. You understand and manage emotional intelligence and promote confidence and encourage determination in self and others. You do not let outraged emotions set you off, nor do you allow over-sensitivity to cloud your judgment of doing what you know is right (morally, ethically, or legally).

To score 9 or 10, you must regularly demonstrate humility, self-correct inappropriate behavior and conversations. You operate calmly. People think of you as approachable, believable, and compassionate.

For a score of 6 or below, you find yourself apologizing frequently for your actions, raising your voice to others, or avoiding taking accountability for your actions.

FORWARD & CRITICAL THINKING

1   2   3   4   5   6   7   8   9   10

Your thoughts include both short- and long-term objectives. A forward-thought leader uses skills: observation, analysis, interpretation, reflection, evaluation and inference, explanation, problem-solving, and decision-making. You are hopeful and optimistic of the future.

To score 9 or 10, you have participated in the evaluation of political, economic, social, and technology trends and mapped scenarios for strategic planning.

For a score of 6 or below, you tend to get trapped by the past and are afraid to take risks. You look over your shoulder frequently, worrying about what might happen if something goes wrong.

GOAL SETTING

1 2 3 4 5 6 7 8 9 10

You look to the future and set objectives with a balance of reasonability yet stretch. You set big, hairy, audacious outcomes and try your best to attain them.

To score a 9 or 10, your goals have been put into written form (paper or digital). You have set a minimum of 3 goals for yourself and you monitor the goals periodically. At least one of your goals is about personal development.

For a score of 6 or under, you have not set any goals or you set goals but have not reviewed them in any reasonable timeframe. Your goals fail to meet the SMART goal formula (Specific | Measurable | Attainable | Relevant |Time-based).

INNOVATION & CREATIVITY

1 2 3 4 5 6 7 8 9 10

You identify needs and participate (individually or collectively) in a process to solve them. You challenge the status quo and ask, "Why do we do it this way?" You approach problem-solving with the intention to be more efficient, effective, have a competitive advantage, or reduce social strife and inequities.

To score a 9 or 10, your solutions benefit others first, and self is second. You have contributed to one of these types of innovation: product, service, process, management, open, and business model.

For a score of 6 and below, you are more resistant to change. You tend to be a protector of the past and justify why things have always been done that way. You try to be clever, crafty, or sassy with your solutions, and they fail to solve a need. You believe that only creative and innovative people solve big corporate, personal, or social issues or concerns.

NEGOTIATION SKILLS

1 2 3 4 5 6 7 8 9 10

You work toward a common promise (compromise) for all involved. Through negotiation, you demonstrate a high degree of acumen in these areas: communication, persuasion, planning, strategizing, and cooperating.

To score a 9 or 10, you understand problem analysis to identify interests and goals, prepare before a meeting, practice active listening, keep your emotions in check, offer clear and effective communication, and encourage collaboration and teamwork.

To score a 6 or below, you need to argue more about your position and less about resolving a disagreement. You cannot be impartial to the subject because you are too emotionally charged about the subject matter. You have abruptly ended an encounter because it was not going your way or you were tired of what you deemed "nonsense" and don't get paid enough to put up with that.

CONFLICT RESOLUTION

1 2 3 4 5 6 7 8 9 10

You seek a peaceful solution between two opposing forces that each party can agree to, work as quickly to resolve as possible, and improve, not damage, the relationship between individuals and groups involved in the conflict.

To score a 9 or 10, you have met these 4 criteria: a) understood the conflict, b) communicated with honesty and candor, c) kept an open mind, and d) coped with the stress and pressure tactics without losing your cool.

For a score of 6 or below, you often find yourself the subject of conflict, are the last one to agree to resolve, or avoid conflicts and leave the mess for others to fix.

ANALYTICAL SKILLS

1   2   3   4   5   6   7   8   9   10

You follow a typical process to separate information into small, bite-sized pieces with the intent to draw conclusions. You demonstrate a high degree of logical reasoning without emotional discourse. You collect data, analyze recurring themes or trends in the information, formulate solutions, and make decisions.

To score 9 or 10, you demonstrate these characteristics: curiosity, fact-seeking, and process-driven.

For a score of 6 or below, you cannot make up your mind on a course of action because the amount of data is too overwhelming. You feel paralyzed to make a decision as you spend too much time collecting and researching data.

SMARTIES CANDY AND SUPERPOWERS

"Look, Mom. I can fly!"

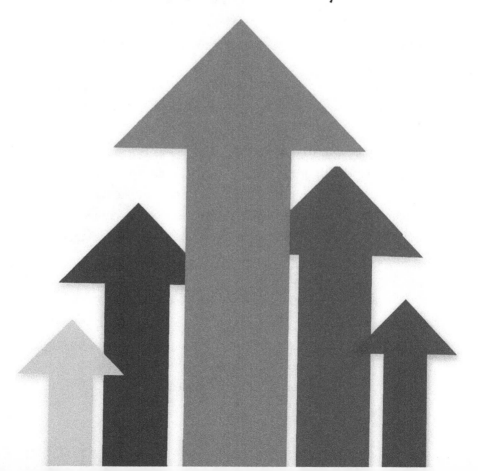

"DREAMS BECOME VISIONS WHEN ONE IS AWAKENED INTO ACTION."

THIS IS THE QUOTE I use during a mentoring session focused on innovation and creativity. First, it is essential to note how a dreamer and a visionary look at a situation or a problem that requires a resolution. For me, dreaming is a state of mind where the eyes are closed. The mind is wandering, fixated upon the puzzle, riddle, or need to be solved. You view it from various angles, keeping in mind that the solutions may be found either inside or outside of the box. Visions require the eyes to be open, and your body is in motion working in the present toward the hope of a future using existing materials on hand or inventing new tools or resources.

Secondly, translating dreams and visions to the creative process comes next. In my experience, dreams are the moments when we are standing still wishing for something, and visions are the time we are thrust into motion toward the future. Mom would tell me that my imagination was only limited by the ability to transform a dream into a vision. She encouraged me to put my imagination to work finding innovative and creative solutions to problems or challenging opportunities. When I am in the dream state, my eyes are closed and the mind is free to wander. Dreams are powerful mental images that evoke emotions, ideas, and sometimes sensations. Visions fuel our ability to create and imagine possibilities, as we say "beyond our wildest dreams." In dreams, logic no longer has control. Your mind is free to explore and expose feelings and experiences that the conscious mind will not. It is here that your creative tendencies take shape and, when recalled, provide inspiration for innovation and art.

To complete the creative process, as Fanny suggested, "Dreams must become visions." Meaning that we take the idea from the unconscious and move it to the conscious. It goes from being a wish to a future hope. As visionaries, we use our imagination to spark an ability to reimagine, retool, and reinvent an idea or concept. In essence, the dream is used to spark the vision. Mom said I could be anything I wanted to be, or could create whatever I wanted, if I genuinely believed it was possible and began to take action to achieve it.

Problems that need solving begin with a process. That's how your innovative tendencies are engaged. You start by finding a specific and desired need that serves a greater good—either for an individual or a collective group of people. These needs may be finding ways for teams to work more cohesively while at the same time developing consumer products. Or possibly discovering new methods of agriculture, offering unconventional transportation alternatives, or finding solutions that resolve civil and social injustices or disparities.

Once the need is defined, begin to ask questions and discover its root cause. Then collect data, review trends, and understand what has been done to solve this problem in the past. Through analysis, apply various solutions to the problem and determine which provides the most effective outcome. This is how one innovates. Innovative solutions don't need to be "bigger than life." Nor do they need to be something that rivals curing a disease, making a huge scientific discovery, or ending world conflict. Being innovative simply requires one to find an answer that addresses a problem or concern at hand. When someone is focused solely on creativity through craftiness or cleverness, but it doesn't solve a problem, that's called *art*.

No problem is too great, so "put your mind to it and you can do it." Yet Fanny cautioned that the desire was not enough; it would merely be a start. It would be important to remain teachable, keep an open mind, and commit to putting that knowledge into action to give my dreams life as a vision.

When it's time for action, the eyes are wide open. You have a laser focus on the prize, even if you're not yet sure what it is. The intention is to look in the direction of the vision, that place just ahead of what is out of reach—that something that can be nearly seen in a conceptual or physical form of what lies ahead.

Finding successful outcomes takes imagination, the desire to dream without inhibition, and the courage to take action on a path toward a vision. Visions must rely on creativity, imagination, and innovation and will become perfectly aligned when one:

Aspires toward the vision.

Thinks without boundaries.

Keeps my eyes wide open.

Takes action based on the options.

MAKING SOMETHING NEW FROM SOMETHING OLD

MOM LOVED TO SEW quilts and knit afghans. She also made crafts out of used items from around the house and tried to incorporate purple, her favorite color, every chance possible. Often, I would find her nestled in the big blue armchair that was a hand-me-down from Aunt Millie, trying to solve puzzles, especially word searches. Mom also loved to bake and was skilled at making homemade bread, biscuits, and cakes. Her specialty—and what she was known for—became Grandma Frances' green cookies.

She enjoyed using her mind and believed that exercising her brain would keep it strong and healthy. Unfortunately, later in life, she was stricken with Alzheimer's, and all her preparation would be to no avail. The dangerous effects of dementia stole her memories and severely reduced her abilities to think cognitively and speak with ease. Alzheimer's affects the neurons and their networks, causing a gap in short-term memories and the inability of her body to repair damaged brain cells through sleep. This disease severely impacts one's communication skills and impedes important and critical metabolic processes that help people thrive on a daily basis.

Mom's love of crafts didn't start out as a hobby. For her, it started as a necessity to help make ends meet. Our town had no department stores or supermarkets, so driving down the street to buy what we needed wasn't an option. It was a thirty-minute drive one way to go shopping, so those trips were limited.

In those days, we lived by the saying, "Invention is the mother of necessity." This became especially handy when it came to decorating our Christmas tree. We made our own ornaments out of pinecones, discarded styrofoam, and leftover Christmas cards. Fanny said, "We are going to be creative on a penny and make people think we spent a dime." Mom was a craft magician. She could use items that usually would be discarded and bring them back to life in a new way. I suspect this mindset was part of the impact she experienced growing up during the Great Depression.

We made our own gifts, too. "Gifts made from love, especially to another person's liking, will be cherished and remembered for a long time to come," she would say. As you can imagine, our gifts fell into two categories: practical and budget conscious. Mom definitely knew how to make a shiny penny look like a dime.

Mom was known in the neighborhood for her craftiness. One year, she even found a way to take the fronts of the previous year's Christmas cards and cut them into pieces using a pattern. She punched holes on the three sides and stitched them together using red yarn to make bowls. Mom would fill them with nuts or her famous biscuit-like sugar cookies. Each bowl was unique, and they became a popular neighborhood favorite for years to come.

My favorite at-home craft day included Mom and me making a paper dog for Grandma Goldie and Robbie the Robot for my brother using items we had on hand. I was excited to be part of the project and offered to use the chore money I had earned. Once we figured out what we would need, it was time to go into town. At Woolworth's Five & Dime we bought the additional craft items, including:

Five shiny pennies in my pocket

Four spools of black thread

Three nifty buttons

Two bright yellow and green dishcloths, and

A bright blue scouring pad for dishes.

When we returned home, supplies in hand, I also gathered up one roll of paper towels and a roll of toilet paper from our supply. Then the process of making a paper dog began. The roll of paper towels was used as the body, supported by four spools of thread. We used the roll of toilet paper for the head, and the scouring pad was shoved inside the cardboard opening to make a nose. Tying the dishcloth around the body and the roll of toilet paper held the paper dog's head in place. The ends of the ties served as his ears. Finishing touches included using buttons and leftover felt scraps to make two black eyes and a bright red tongue. The second dishcloth was placed into the cardboard opening of the paper towels to form its tail. When Grandma carefully unwrapped her gift, the look on her face was priceless!

Next up was the making of Robbie the Robot. Mom stepped aside and allowed Dad and me to work on this project together since most of the supplies would come from Dad's garage.

Before heading out to his workbench, we grabbed two empty Pringles cans and several small boxes that would be the body of the robot. The garage always smelled of oil from the mechanical work Dad did beyond his regular job. Today, that smell brings back a rush of memories of that time. Dad guided me through the process of building Robbie and helped me to secure the legs with tape and use the boxes to make the robot's body and head.

We rolled two pieces of old, heavy electrical wire to form movable arms and slid them into the body. The robot's hands were made by attaching a clothespin at the end of each coiled wire. The rest of the robot was constructed using leftover bolts and scraps in Dad's garage. Robbie, the robot, got a fresh coat of silver paint, and he was finished.

These craft experiences expanded my imagination. Fanny taught me to see the treasures others considered useless and trash and use them in new ways. I learned that when you use your brain to solve problems or seek effective outcomes, you may have to look in unconventional places or visualize objects from different angles to stimulate innovation and creativity. The ability to apply my thinking in this way has shaped my understanding that sometimes what you make as new has come from something old.

 ## THE GREEN COOKIE EFFECT

MOM DIDN'T SEEK OUT opportunities to be "important" or known for something spectacular. She just did what she thought was needed and did so with a high degree of integrity, commitment, and determination.

Many of us have fond memories of going to Grandma's house, especially during the holidays. We enter the home, and the smell of something baking in the oven or simmering on the stove entices our sense of smell, further magnified by the visual appeal and tastiness. The familiar sounds of chicken frying in the cast iron skillet or the timer going off just as the perfectly browned turkey comes out of the oven reaches our ears. Immediately, imagining how it tastes and wanting to sit down and dig in right away. We pick up the fried chicken wing, double dipped in egg yolk and coated in flour infused with cornstarch, grab that first sliver of turkey breast, or sneak a cookie like no one is going to notice. The final sensation of our food experience happens when all five senses come together with a bang.

Creativity, innovation, and imagination are aided by our senses, whether we have or use all five or not. They are entwined in how we react to our world. Our senses help us shape our impressions and perceptions of our experiences. That's how it happened with Grandma Frances' green cookies. Mom used Aunt Millie's sugar cookie recipe as her batter. Her unique twist was using buttermilk in place of regular milk to mix the ingredients. Then the trick was to limit touching the dough as little as possible with your hands or rolling pin. After the mixture was complete, she spread flour on the wood cutting board and carefully laid the cookie dough on top of the flour. Watching her knead the dough was like seeing a machine in action.

Flip, knead, press.

Another flip and knead again.

Press the dough as flat as possible.

Mom used a wide-mouthed canning jar and a diamond-shaped tin cookie cutter to form her cookies. I'd like to say she chose those shapes because her cookies were over the moon and more precious than diamonds, but that would be an author embellishing his story. Each cookie was tenderly placed on a large, Crisco-smothered cookie sheet and popped in the oven. The timer was set. Several minutes later emerged the most fantastically tasting, biscuit-like sugar cookies one would ever see, smell, touch, or taste. These cookies literally melted in your mouth. They were thick and flaky, not like the thin and crisp versions sold in stores. To top off her delectable treat, Mom mixed butter and a portion of buttermilk with confectionery sugar (powdered sugar) to make the icing. For variety, she placed the icing in separate bowls and added food coloring before scooping her freshly made sweetness on top of each cookie.

After the grandchildren came along, Mom continued her cookie-making tradition. On one particular day, the strangest thing happened. The cookies covered in yellow, red, and blue were left on the plate. It was the green cookies that were gobbled up! What surprised us most that day was that we realized Mom never topped the cookies with purple-colored icing—purple being her favorite color. Our second surprise, and what we came to learn, was that the kids thought the cookies with the green icing tasted better. Fanny, not wanting to be the one to disappoint, whipped up another batch, and every cookie had an ample topping of green icing. The grandkids fondly deemed them "Grandma Frances' Green Cookies."

That day, Mom could have argued with the kids or told them

that all the icings were the same, just the coloring was different, but she didn't want to take away the magic of the experience. And even though the adults wanted to interject comments about the taste of the icing, Mom would not hear it. She shushed us with her finger and that eye of hers, the one I had come to know all so well. Mom did this in the name of making the green cookies famous by a whole new generation.

Mom saw no value in taking away their perception of what they liked, even if it was imaginary. Instead, she retooled her approach and chose the cookie color that appealed to their tastebuds. When one is trying to apply innovation and creativity, the point is to find a solution that works for those who have the need. It's not to create something that makes the leader look good or serves only his or her needs. Mom made one subtle change, without too much effort on her part, to please the "customer." Not all solutions require a sophisticated or complex approach. In my mind, I see this as an application of Fanny's lesson about looking for answers outside the box. She would be quick to remind me that there are times when what you're looking for is just a new way of seeing the box. This is how it works in business, too. As leaders, we must be aware that some of the most innovative and creative solutions require the simplest of tweaks to make them a successful outcome.

When I asked Mom why she didn't tell the kids that they all tasted the same, Fanny took the cookie I was about to eat. She held it, looked at me over the top of her glasses, and said, "Why would I want to spoil their imagination over the icing color? It's not always about being right." Then she smiled, took a bite, and handed me back my green cookie.

IMAGINATION IS YOUR
GREATEST SUPERPOWER

DURING MY EARLY CHILDHOOD, even though our neighborhood was full of kids, one of my favorite pastimes was playing with my imaginary friends. You could always count on these friends. They never got mean, took your toys, or had to go home at the end of the day. It was my invisible friends who kept me company most often. We played hoops, kicked the ball against the garage, and dug holes in the dirt with my special backhoe named Mary Ann. I'm not sure how that name came about, although I did have a crush on the *Gilligan's Island* farm girl of the same name.

One of my favorite pastimes was inventing superpowers. As far as I can remember, it started with watching Saturday morning cartoons. Tarzan and Batman were my heroes. Pounding my arms on my chest, I would give out a screeching yell that would cause all the animals of the jungle to assist me on any adventure I could imagine. My screeching became so annoying that Mom suggested I go to the top of the hill the next time I had the urge to call the animals because apparently she had seen some elephants, tigers, and monkeys near the large maple tree. At the time, her suggestion seemed to make sense. I was pretty forceful, probably more likely—just loud.

At Halloween one year, after my brother and I had come home from trick-or-treat, we were left with almost a full bag of Smarties candy, which Mom said I could have. These are small, sugary pellets that come in different colors and flavors bound in a plastic wrapper that is self-twisted on each end. As I ate the candy over the next couple of weeks, an idea popped into my head. *What if each of the five colors evoked a superpower? This would be so cool.*

It took me a while to decide which color would have their very own superpower. I started with Green since it was one of my favorite colors. Green was for invisibility. To make the power work, I stood against the wall, popped the pellet into my mouth, and let it dissolve. Once it was gone, I placed my hands over my eyes and stood motionless, trying not to breathe. It worked. Mom would go by me several times and wonder where I had gone. She would go to the back screen door and yell outside for me to come in. She looked for me under the table, behind Aunt Millie's armchair, and in the hall closet. Then she'd come really close to me. I could feel her right there and would yell my name. It always made me giggle, but I never moved my hands. After another minute or so, Mom would start touching the wall close to me until she finally put her hand on my head. "There you are," she'd say with a smile.

For some reason, my invisible superpower only worked on Mom. My brother always found me right away. I figured out that he had taken the white Smarties. Its powers canceled out all the others.

My brother and I played outdoors a lot when we were kids. Mom thought it was good for us to be in the fresh air, where we had lots of space to explore, run wild, and even ride motorbikes from time to time. On the days when it was freezing cold, snowing, or raining, we would stay indoors and watch TV. That was a treat, certainly not a right. I was fascinated with the TV show *Batman* and would watch it every chance possible. This was not a cartoon, like the one on Saturday morning with Superman. This Batman was the real deal—a living breathing human being on screen. Back outside with my invisible friends around me, we enacted several fight scenes involving the Caped Crusader and his sidekick, Robin. Together they solved riddles, escaped from ropes and time bombs, and won every fight.

POW.

ZAP.

Holy cow, Batman!

I never had a cape, bat belt, or "batarangs." But I did have Smarties candy, and they gave me superpowers. Surely my abilities would be no match for the Joker, Riddler, Penguin, or Catwoman. Through a series of what can only be explained as imagination on steroids,

I decided that my character needed to fly. So, with the help of my blue Smarties, the color for flying, and the umbrella I stole from the Penguin, I climbed the ladder next to the back porch. Looking over the side, it seemed like a long way down—I was just a little scared. Neither Tarzan, Batman, nor Superman ever looked like they were scared of anything. Tarzan could fly through the jungle, Batman flew in a helicopter, and Superman soared through the sky. I opened the umbrella, placed a blue Smarties in my mouth, closed my eyes, and jumped.

Straight down.

In no time.

Plop on the ground.

Laying there in shock and amazement, my thoughts were, "How could this be?" I had seen this happen so perfectly on TV. This must be a bad batch of candy. Mom came running outside, thanks to my brother tattling on me. I laid on the ground with several brightly colored Smarties strewn in the grass. My very sad-looking umbrella was shaped like it had just been caught in a windstorm and turned inside out.

Fortunately, I was okay. No broken bones, only bruised pride. Mom helped me wipe away my tears and sat me up. She hugged me for what seemed like ages. It was as if that moment had been frozen in time. In my strongest yet quivering voice, I told her, "Quick, find the pink Smarties. (sniff, sniff) It has the power to heal me." She humored me and administered my sugary medicine, then she took my face into her hands. Mom was so loving and gentle. Again, she kissed my forehead as she had done so many times before. That's when Fanny told me, "Superheroes are made from the inside out."

Mom reminded me that my greatest power will always come from within myself. She pressed her hand against my chest. "It is the love you have for others and yourself that will be your greatest power. One day when you grow up, you'll understand more of what I am saying. Just know that you won't need these candies to give you courage, strength, or powers to do what's right." We sat there without moving and talked about my adventure. I apologized multiple times for making her worry about me.

With an encouraging tone, Mom suggested I use my imagination a little differently. She encouraged me to think and play creatively but find ways that would not scare the bejesus out of her. Fanny put her arm around me and walked me inside for a quick snack. Along the way, she gave me three instructions:

1. Keep my feet firmly on the ground.
2. Only use my superpowers in the house.
3. Don't pull another stunt like that again, or she would eat a whole package of Smarties candy and finish me herself.

I got the point. The blue Smarties would be retired when playing outside. However, she had no idea how much power the orange one possessed—a story for another time.

→ EVEN THE BEST-MADE PLANS

AS I MENTIONED EARLIER, Mom and Dad's favorite pastimes were camping and fishing, which seem to have had even more meaning to them after Mom recovered from cancer. Almost every weekend, from the beginning of March through the middle of October, we'd pack up the camper with all sorts of games and supplies and head to one of several campsites we favored.

After V and I were married, and before we had children of our own, we often joined Mom and Dad on their camping adventures. It was always fun getting away. Mom and Dad loved to try new gadgets. On one trip, they had just purchased a Quickie Piemaker. It was a double-sided cast iron, round pie maker that held two pieces of bread and toppings in between the slices. After placing the buttered bread and fillings together, the Quickie Piemaker would be clamped and placed in the fire to toast the bread and heat up the filling.

We had so much fun using our imagination and creativity to make desserts, sandwiches, and even our version of a calzone. Anything that we could think of to put between two pieces of bread was possible. One of the downsides of the maker was the cleanup. The fillings often oozed out of the sides and would burn onto the cast-iron mold. We'd have to wait for it to cool down before we attempted to clean it, which made it even harder to remove what had adhered to the sides of the mold.

One day I had a brilliant idea. Why not put the Quickie Piemaker back into the campfire after cooking and let the heat dissolve any remaining burnt pieces? This would make the clean up a snap. So, without further ado, the maker was thrust back onto the hot coals. Time passed, and I had forgotten about the maker in the fire. Mom suggested that maybe it was time to take it out. I went over and grabbed the wood handles of the Quickie Piemaker and pulled it out of the fire.

No burnt and crusty pieces.

No cast-iron molds, either.

Only two sticks with wood handles left.

The coals were so hot they melted the cast iron mold right off the ends of the metal sticks. We laughed so hard that our sides and faces hurt. From that moment on, whenever anyone had a bright idea, we would say it wasn't nearly as bright as my idea to clean the maker.

Fanny gave me an "A" for ingenuity and an "F" for execution. I knew Mom and Dad had just purchased the Quickie Piemaker from the camper store. They weren't the type to just buy things, so I knew they spent money from their camping fund. Although it didn't cost much by today's standards, I mailed them a check to replace the new maker's cost. On our next excursion, Dad proudly displayed two roasting sticks perfect for cooking hot dogs or roasting marshmallows. Mom suggested that I should cook but leave the cleanup for her.

We had lots of fun retelling the story of the maker, and with each version, we embellished more and more, making it funnier every time we told it. Instead of being the "big to bigger fish" story, it was the "Night the Quickie Piemaker went out somewhere not in Georgia."

It wasn't until I was cleaning out old papers Mom and Dad left behind after their passing that I discovered one more fact about the Quickie Piemaker incident. In between a clear plastic sleeve was my original check I sent them to replace the maker. Mom had never cashed it. Beside the check was a note in Mom's handwriting: "In memory of my smart little boy who has grown to be a man with the heart of a leader."

TEACHABLE MOMENTS

- Make something new from something old—there are times when we must reimagine how we think so we can retool and reinvent solutions with minimal expense.
- Green Cookie Effect—not every problem requires a sophisticated or complex solution. Sometimes when we seek "out-of-the-box thinking," we need to consider the answer may very well be the box itself.
- Imagination is your greatest superpower—the spirit of innovation is sparked by the encouragement to have a child's imagination, although we are supposed to be "all grown up." Innovation is bringing forth a solution that meets a specific need. It is a fresh idea or perspective that is formed from scratch or an enhancement to something that is made better.
- Even the best-made plans—not everything goes exactly as we thought it might. But that shouldn't keep us from trying. When things don't work out, be responsible and accountable. Then step back up to the plate, or get back on that horse, as these colloquial sayings imply, and do it again.

For your free *Fanny Rules* Teachable Moments Journal go to https://drtroyhall.com/documents/fannyrulesjournal.pdf.

MENTORING LESSONS FOR RULE SIX: INNOVATION AND CREATIVITY

1. Take a moment and think about one person who has encouraged you the most to be imaginative and creative. If that person is still living, write a letter, send an email, or reach out to them and tell them how much you appreciate their support. Should the person you think about is unable to be reached, consider writing a letter anyway to express your thoughts. Putting your thoughts in writing or text is a great way to express your inner feelings and show appreciation and gratitude.

2. Create a vision board that reflects your dreams, visions, and aspirations. Visualizing your dreams has a powerful impact, and seeing words and images increases your chances of achieving those dreams.

   • The vision board is the "power tool" to bring your imagination, innovation, and creativity into focus. Use a poster board or paper (or a digital option) for the foundation of your vision board. Cut out words or images from magazines or other printed materials, add photos, words, or phrases to make a collage of what you want to see in your future. You can follow the same process to make a collage of your vision on your computer if you choose. Simply cut and paste your power words and images from digital sources and make an electronic vision board.

   • On a separate piece of paper (or on your computer), write down the biggest dream you're chasing today.

   • Identify what it would take to make this dream a vision that can become a reality and write that down under your biggest dream.

- Finally, write down how you will feel when this vision becomes a reality. It's generally recommended that this be a statement written in the present tense...so, for example, "Now that I have _____, I feel _____."

CLEAN YOUR ROOM WHETHER IT NEEDS IT OR NOT

"It's not the successes or failures that shape your life, it's how you handle them."

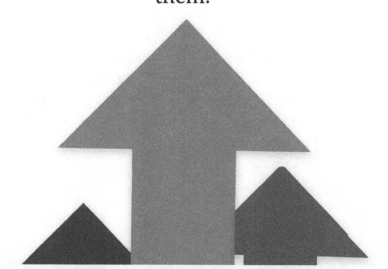

"FAILURE IS SIMPLY PART OF THE JOURNEY—NOT THE DESTINATION."

FANNY COACHED ME TO WORK hard and be disciplined in all I did. She pushed me to allow my determination to give me the edge to fight for what I wanted to accomplish and how I wanted to be remembered. Her advice was simple: *when you fail, get back up and try again.* She wanted me to have a firmness of purpose and let that be my guide to try again.

A reporter once asked Thomas Edison how he felt about his light bulb experiment failing one thousand times. In Edison's response, he indicated the light bulb did not fail one thousand times; it took one thousand steps to become a success. Although Mom did not know Edison, she shared his perspective and never kept score of what was a success and what was a failure. She focused solely on how failure was simply part of the journey and not the destination. Our greatest achievements are often built on failure, defeat, and even catastrophe when we dare to get back up and try again.

Few would argue that many of us have the fortitude and rigor to withstand the many attempts needed to succeed. Yet our discipline and determination are exactly what is needed to stand tall in the face of criticism, mockery, or disbelief in one's ideas. The Great Practice Myth claims that it takes ten thousand hours of application of a skill to be considered an expert in a subject.

Mom would say that brushing my teeth, making my bed, and putting my clothes away were essential tasks to develop my abilities to exercise self-determination. She further emphasized that being regimented and diligent in performing routine tasks would help me remain focused on achieving my dreams, goals, and aspirations creatively. Fanny said, "Cleaning my room whether it needed it or not would build strong character."

Hard work pays off.

Never give up.

No easy way to success.

Mom knew my perseverance would give me the gumption to stick to my future wishes and desires, even when I simply wanted to give up. She also stood firm in the belief that I would eventually develop discipline and determination through creating habits of completing routine chores like making the bed, sweeping the floor, organizing the closet, and cleaning my room. I can assure you that I have devoted more than ten thousand hours to these tasks in my lifetime, which makes me a "skilled expert" in cleaning my room, folding my clothes, and making my bed, to name a few.

Painful or not, executing these types of tasks has a lasting effect that contributes to success. Therefore, as potentially irrelevant as they may seem to a teenager, training oneself to complete these mundane but essential jobs develops muscle memory for the brain. This type of memory is the one recalled to help a person overcome obstacles even when they seem too large to manage.

Fanny often told me, "Failures build character, and success is its reward." She helped me realize that discipline and determination, the emotional feeling gained when staying focused on a difficult goal, were my strengths. I can still hear her words today.

"Never give up."

"You can do it."

"Believe in yourself."

"Persevere."

Those mundane but important habits are still with me today. Before heading to work or play—weekdays or weekends—I make my bed and tidy my space, embracing a quiet sense of accomplishment, looking back into the room before pulling the door closed. These simple habits were the stepping stones to acquiring self-discipline. No matter how tired or hurried, I am determined to keep the streak alive by doing these chores every day, embracing the self-confidence I've built from adhering to Fanny's Rules. For that, I am grateful and thankful.

BE PROUD OF YOUR WORK

FANNY COUNSELED ME, "Keep your pride to yourself." She knew that my self-determination and rigor to follow processes and obey rules would one day result in outstanding work. Putting a lid on how I felt about my achievements, however, was excellent mentoring advice that would serve me well in the years to come. Accolades bestowed on me from others would taste sweeter than if I had served up the compliments myself.

I see this as an extension of her Step Ladder wisdom shared in Rule Two when Fanny cautioned that the people I saw on my way to the top would be the same people I'd encounter on my way back down. Although she was happy to hear I wasn't planning to step on anyone to get ahead, Fanny knew that if I allowed pride in my accomplishments to become the center of my speaking, I would be leaving an unwanted footprint on those around me.

Mom's instructions were clear: let others be proud of you. When pride in oneself is outwardly expressed, it can be interpreted as dishonest, untrustworthy, disingenuous, or unbelievable. Her belief was that an outward expression of pride could signal feelings of superiority, arrogance, or inordinate self-esteem. Pride rarely has a positive connotation. In those instances, pride may be conveyed as a sense of accomplishment or pleasure in one's possessions. But that is such a fine line. One that is best not to step on it or cross over.

On the flip side, Fanny wanted me to be proud of my work and instructed me to do my very best in everything. However, to achieve a level of distinction and let people know you take your work seriously:

Put forth a reasonable effort.

Challenge yourself beyond the status quo.

Strive for high levels of performance, not perfection.

"You put your best before God and man, not your halfway, or some ill-performed attempt to just get by. Go all the way, or don't go at all. Be either hot or cold. There is no room for being lukewarm." Fanny added, "There was a reason Jesus spit lukewarm out of his mouth." Being so-so was settling for a mediocre performance. If you want to be known for greatness, then work through whatever gets in your way. Do it with zest and vigor, and if you've laid it all out, then you can be proud of what you have accomplished. To get the best, you must put forth your best. Mediocre never rises to the top. It settles for the bottom then complains about the view.

My niece, who I mentioned earlier in Rule Four, recalled a specific instance when Fanny laid out how she could take pride in what she did while balancing marriage, family, and work at the same time. It went something like this:

> "Have internal pride in your work. If you are going to take the time to do it, then do it right the first time. Don't expect others to clean up what you couldn't do well from the beginning. When you say you're going to do something, honor your commitment, and get it done. Even though it may be convenient to cancel a promise you made because you just don't feel like doing it or something more fun comes up, fight the urge and do what you said you'd do. Make your word and work have meaning."

 ## EARN THE PURPLE RIBBON

IN THE YOUTH DEVELOPMENT PROGRAM 4-H, blue ribbons are for superior ratings, red ribbons signify average work, and white ones are for a good try. The purple ribbon, however, is the highest award one can achieve. It signals the BEST of the BEST. Typically, when someone mentions 4-H, people think of an animal or livestock competition held in a fair-like venue that promotes the value of farming. 4-H is actually much more than that. The four Hs stand for Head, Heart, Hands, & Health. The organization offers a wide range of youth development activities through inspirational, hands-on learning experiences.

Both V and I were 4-Hers. Actually, the first time I ever saw V was on March 15, 1974, when we attended a regional youth 4-H retreat at Jackson's Mills State Camp in Lewis County, West Virginia. V had the sweetest smile, beautiful almond-shaped eyes, and dark brown hair that fell beyond her shoulders. She was shy and giggly. It was a life-changing weekend and the beginning of getting to know the same person for more than forty-six years.

I had driven to the event. It was one of the rare times Dad let me take his 1969 Volkswagen Beetle on an overnight stay. As the weekend came to a close, I waited until all the attendees were picked up by their parents. I planned to spend some extra time with this girl, especially since she seemed interested in me. Hopefully, we would have some time to talk outside the cabins.

It was a little chilly that afternoon. The cool mountain breeze hid the flushness that was in my cheeks. I stood next to V dressed in my band jacket with my hands neatly tucked in my pockets. It was hard to tell if they were sweating because I was more focused on the fact that my heart was racing one hundred miles per minute.

V was donned in what was fashionably known at the time as a purple maxi-coat. It was an ankle-length covering made of wool, which buttoned up the front and supported a big collar. As we awkwardly talked about the weather and some of the weekend's activities, another burst of air whistled by us. I am the more outgoing of the two of us, but for some reason, I acted like the cowardly lion, without a brain and a beating heart that would have made the tin man rattle louder than a farm tractor pulling a load of hay.

At the moment, V, as uncharacteristically as she had told me many years afterward, mustered up the courage to ask me if I wanted to sit beside her on the stone steps. I became a bumbling idiot and was unable to put words into a string of coherent thought. My inside voice kept saying,

"What are you thinking?"

"Go for it."

"It's not every day you get an offer like this."

I then said something that resembled, "It would be too cold to sit on the stone steps." With a determined motion, V opened her maxi-coat, flung one edge of it over the stone next to her, and exclaimed, "You can sit on my purple coat."

All the way home, I kept replaying this encounter in my mind, trying to remember every detail so I could share it with Mom. After parking the Beetle in her spot next to the garage and descending from Cloud Nine, I hurried past Dad, who was tinkering on his truck, and ran inside to tell Mom all about the weekend. She was at the counter, cutting up tomatoes for that evening's dinner. I was so excited to tell her everything that I forgot to take off my jacket.

Mom listened intently to me talk about my weekend—the skits, field events, and competitions. First, I told her about the purple ribbon I won for public speaking, and second, I told her about the girl. Not just any girl, she was "the girl." (Before pulling the Beetle in the driveway, I had already reached a firm decision that V was the one.) I had never met anyone like my V. She was so sweet and friendly. Seemed shy on the inside, was bright on the outside, and was so darn cute.

This was the one.

Had to be.

I felt the flutter.

When I had finished recounting every detail of the 4-H weekend, Mom turned from the stove where she had been stirring the spaghetti sauce, put down the spoon, and gave me a kiss on the forehead. I could see the twinkle in her eye. Mom knew her son was growing into a young man. She asked when she could meet this special girl. Then it hit me: "How was I going to find her again?" I had been so preoccupied with our encounter that I only managed to get her first name.

Dejected at the thought the woman of my future was going to slip away, I put my hands into my jacket pockets and hung my head to sulk. Inside was a nicely folded piece of paper. I pulled it out. There in clear print, with the biggest, boldest, and best handwriting ever, was her name and phone number. That girl was truly amazing. She had slipped it into my pocket before we left the camp. Fanny's advice,

"Get to know her."

"Let her get to know you."

"Become friends first."

She continued, "Be yourself and be your best. If it's meant to be, it will happen. You'll have a better chance of success if you take her feelings into consideration before your own." As I suspected, Mom injected the subtlety of relationships and how to treat others in some of her first bits of advice to help me connect with the girl I would be with for the rest of my life.

Her most humorous words of wisdom were for me to take it slow. "Ha!" I laughed inside. She told me to watch my pace with the girl who had swung open her coat, offered me a seat on a stone step, and secretly placed her name and phone number on a piece of paper in my jacket pocket.

I was determined to meet this girl again. What would our first date be like? It was so hard to imagine. My excitement mounted as I was now prepared to learn more about the girl wearing a purple maxi-coat. V delivered a purple ribbon performance on the steps of a cabin. On that day, she warmed my heart, and you could say my *fanny*, too.

PINBALL WIZARD

BEFORE ELTON JOHN'S HIT SINGLE "Pinball Wizard" in 1975, I was quite the gamester. During the summer of 1967, we stayed at a campground with a convenience store at the entrance. It was run by

Lou and Nin, who were simple country folks with hearts as large as some of the biggest rainbow trout Dad had ever caught.

Without fail, Lou and Nin made even strangers feel like long-lost friends. The store carried basic food and typical camping supplies, unusually ice-cold bottles of Dr. Pepper, Smarties candy, and ice cream. Tucked neatly into the corner was the most fantastically, musically inspired, colorful, and electric pinball machine. Across from it were a row of stools with red tops for counter service, a bank of wooden booths next to the windows, and a jukebox playing country music.

Using the chore money I had earned, every afternoon I headed to the store to play pinball. I loved whacking the silver ball with the flippers, causing it to bounce off the bumpers and land in the bonus-point valued side compartments and holes. My challenge was scoring enough points to win a free game before losing all five balls or tilting the machine.

At first, I wasn't very good and quickly used up my coins. But that did not stop me. I became even more committed to winning. Persistence and determination fueled my desire to score my first free game. That's when the machine lit up and flashed its bright lights to the sound of what can only be described as the kind of melody you'd hear from an ice cream truck.

Some days, Mom sat on one of the swiveling stools drinking her Dr. Pepper from a straw and watching me play. She could visibly see the intense concentration and determination exuding from my entire body. I was totally committed—body, mind, and soul. It wasn't hard to see how determined I was and that I would not give up until I earned the title of *Pinball Wizard*.

Some of the locals knew Fanny and Slim from fishing with them at the river. They recognized me as the kid with the chubby cheeks and Gilligan-style hat that sat in a lawn chair at the side of the riverbank writing in a journal while my brother collected odd-shaped rocks or chased lizards, grasshoppers, and the occasional snake as Mom and Dad casted their lines, hoping to hook a trout or bass for dinner.

My brother routinely fell asleep in the car on the way back to the campsite, finishing his nap in the car, while Dad skinned the fish from the day's catch and Mom prepped the fire and set the picnic table for dinner. As much as I enjoyed being with them, I couldn't wait to get back to camp and head to the store to play pinball. Within minutes of pulling back into our site, I'd jump out of the car, grab my roll of nickels, and run down the gravel road to Lou and Nin's.

As I entered the store, I'd wave to Lou as I walked quickly toward the pinball machine that was waiting for me in the corner. I'd place a few coins on the glass top and select Player One. Then I'd pull back the tab, release it, and send my first ball into motion.

I was intense.

Determined.

Resolute to win.

For hours, I'd play without stopping and make my nickels last as long as possible. Winning one free game after the other was a rush. Fellow campers would challenge me to beat my previous score. If I did it, they'd give me a nickel. When I lost, I'd have to sit out for five minutes before playing another game.

When it was time for dinner, I'd head back to the site and tell Mom all about the games. She would quietly listen as I explained how the flipper got stuck this one time and I had to hit the side of the machine. We both laughed when I told her one of the balls got stuck in a power-point hole and racked up thousands of points while the machine counted off with a sound similar to winning the jackpot at a casino. It was a familiar scene with assigned roles: I talked, Mom listened.

When I finished my stories, Mom congratulated me on my victory. She was happy that I found enjoyment in playing pinball and complimented me on my determination to be good at the game. On cue, the teachable moment arrived. "You know it's just a game?" she asked.

"Of course," I responded.

"Good," Fanny said. "Because I am expecting you to put as much effort and determination into your schoolwork and chores as you did to win free pinball games."

Mom was direct and to the point. Fair and considerate. She knew that if she positioned her teaching in the right way, I would learn to extend the discipline and determination for winning into achieving other goals and outcomes. It is perfectly okay to integrate fun and work. Just be sure to apply the same level or higher of self-determination and persistence to solving problems, creating effective habits, overcoming obstacles, and sticking to tasks that may be more challenging as I did to playing and winning at pinball.

Who knows, maybe one day I will earn the title of Dr. Pinball Wizard.

TEACHABLE MOMENTS

- Be proud of your work—when your hard work pays off, embrace a sense of accomplishment. Take pride in yourself and accept praise from others for your efforts. Build habits that support your decision to follow standards and protocols; stay focused and committed to reinforcing and building those habits.
- Earn the purple ribbon—be your best self. Avoid mediocrity. Go above and beyond to achieve success. Sometimes it may require you to take a calculated risk and attempt something new and out of your comfort zone.
- Pinball Wizard—take the time to enjoy life and know that you can develop productive habits of discipline and determination through fun and games. Not every lesson in life has to have serious overtones.

For your free *Fanny Rules* Teachable Moments Journal go to https://drtroyhall.com/documents/fannyrulesjournal.pdf.

MENTORING LESSONS FOR RULE SEVEN: DISCIPLINE AND DETERMINATION

Use the following questions as conversation starters in your next coaching session with a friend, colleague, or mentor.

- What does it mean for you to follow rules and a set of protocols?
- If your work involves adhering to standards and protocols, how successful are you following or avoiding them?
- How does self-discipline help you to be determined to achieve your dreams, goals, and aspirations?
- What is the most challenging thing you've accomplished that required you to have the gumption to stick it out, even when you wanted to quit? What kept you going?
- How do you prepare yourself to overcome obstacles?
- What effective habits have you found helpful to increase your self-discipline and determination?
- What happens when your good habits slip? How do you get back up?
- What's one thing you've failed at? Something you've succeeded at? Why are failures significant to achieving success?
- Incorporate the nine simple ways to develop a habit of determination to achieve your goals:
  1. Develop a strength in one particular area.
  2. Hone your skill by learning what you can and put that knowledge in play.
  3. Limit your options and do not become distracted on other awards along the way.
  4. Stay in your lane. Remain focused.

5. Meditate on the truth.
6. Learn from the past.
7. Adjust your priorities as often as needed.
8. Create a plan.
9. See yourself winning the prize.

WHO IS YOUR JIMINY CRICKET?

"Being a real boy takes more than a Blue Fairy wish."

OFTEN YOUNG PROFESSIONALS ASK ME FOR LEADERSHIP ADVICE ON HOW TO SUCCEED.

MY RESPONSE? "Get a mentor. It's one of the best gifts you will ever give yourself." Mentoring is a form of coaching between two people. One person serves as the mentor and offers sage advice based on expertise and background. Think of this individual's role as being an added conscience for the other person. The second individual, the mentee, enters the mentoring relationship generally eager and willing to learn from the sage instructor.

While the primary goal of mentoring is to promote career development, it has excellent value shaping the mentee to become successful in other roles in life, such as a valued spouse, conscientious parent, considerate sibling, trained athlete, or a lucrative artist perhaps. One of my mom's greatest gifts was her desire and capacity to serve as my mentor. Fanny's insight and counsel are the lessons behind the making of a leader and why writing this book was essential to me.

When I was a young boy, Mom would read me the story of *Pinocchio*. Geppetto, the puppeteer, wanted to transform his prized wooden puppet into a real boy. Although the plot is unclear on this topic, it makes sense that Geppetto wanted his creation to have life and to interact with him, as he did not have any children. Before going to sleep, Geppetto wished upon a star ruled by the Blue Fairy and she granted the puppeteer his wish, bringing Pinocchio to life. But he wasn't a *real* boy just yet. Pinocchio had to first prove himself as:

Brave.

Truthful.

Unselfish.

To help guide the wooden puppet, the Blue Fairy assigns Jiminy Cricket as his conscience. Jiminy was Pinocchio's mentor.

Looking back now to my time at Mom's bedside when she had cancer, I can see that our relationship was somewhat like that of

Jiminy Cricket and Pinocchio. Of course, Mom was much better looking than an umbrella-toting green insect with a black top hat, suit, and tie and big shoes.

Although I possessed a high capacity for learning, I did not always put all of Fanny's wisdom to use on the first try. She knew it was a journey of self-discovery. Just like Jiminy offered counsel to Pinocchio, Fanny did the same for me. As in the story and how it is often in real life, the coach can only guide the mentee—it is always up to the mentee to make good choices. As Fanny put it, "Character is defined by choices, not circumstances." No matter how much the mentor may want the mentee to make the best choice, in the end, it is always the mentee's option to exercise free will.

During the story, Jiminy tries to motivate Pinocchio to become a courageous, honest, and considerate boy. He attempts to influence the wooden puppet to make good choices of character. Alas, Pinocchio does not heed Jiminy's advice and finds himself trapped in Stromboli's Puppet Show and then again on Pleasure Island.

Ideally, the mentor-mentee relationship creates a learning environment that stimulates critical thinking, develops emotional intelligence, and hones problem-solving skills. When the mentor commits to another's success, they are engaged in the act of transformation. That is the value of mentoring and why it is an essential part of helping one become their best self ever. Mentoring allows for the safe exchange of information, fosters collaboration, and when the two are in sync, it gives to each other more than what the other received.

For years beyond the days of bedside wisdom, Fanny continued to offer insights and guidance. She helped me become the type of leader that would:

- Be teachable, humble, and compassionate with a willingness to extend grace to others for no other reason than because I said so.

- Seek truth from good, reliable sources such as the voices of trusted advisors, counselors, and grounded research data.
- Seek purity of heart, which starts with having good intentions and making decisions for the good of many and not my selfish desires.
- Strive to make peace in all I did and invite others to common ground and common promises.

As referenced in Rule One, these effective-leader attributes, when used in tandem, promote the betterment of the one for the many they will serve. I have realized the importance of a leader's mindset focusing on "being, seeking, and striving" for positive results. This way of thinking supports healthy individual and group relations and demonstrates transformative principles that bring forth success for the mentor and the mentee.

PUPPET ON A STRING

FOLLOW THE LEADER and other games, such as Simon Says and Mother May I, were how my brother and I occupied much of our time together outside. We loved having control over the other when it was time to be the leader. What made the games even more fun was conjuring up superpowers from a fresh batch of Smarties candy and washing them down with a swig of Dr. Pepper.

To some degree, the game Follow the Leader reminds me of what it might have been like to be Pinocchio. Before he was granted individual movement, Geppetto controlled the wooden figure with strings. Every move Pinocchio made was set in motion by someone else. To move an arm or a leg, to make him sit, walk or run, Geppetto pulled strings.

In the Follow the Leader game, the one in charge moves around in the space, and the follower has to mimic the leader's actions.

Sometimes Mom joined in on the fun. When it was her turn to take control, she would go all out and move her arms and legs in crazy motions while twirling around. The three of us would parade around in the yard, jumping, skipping, and doing Tarzan yells.

When Mom let loose, she would have us laughing hysterically. So much so that Dad would lift his head out from under the hood of the truck to see what funny dance moves Mom was making. Mom would...

Look at him.

Put her thumbs to her ears with her fingers spread out like antlers.

Stick out her tongue.

Of course, we would follow suit. Dad would grin, waving his greasy hand at our antics, and go right back to tinkering with the engine.

In business, with every move a leader makes, the employees imitate them accurately. Imagine what my childhood version of Follow the Leader might look like in a work environment—skipping the crazy movements, hands like antlers, and tongues sticking out of people's mouths. As much fun as it was in the backyard hopping on one leg with my hands on my head while screaming to the top of my lungs, that wouldn't translate well in an organization. That's not precisely what is meant to lead by example.

Leaders must be effective role models. It is a reasonable expectation for those in charge to demonstrate the type of behavior others would want to emulate. Often, these types of leaders don't hesitate to jump in and help with a task or project. They subscribe to the maxim that they wouldn't ask someone to do something they would not do themselves. Effective leaders understand that actions speak louder than words. When giving instruction, remember that people do not always remember what you said but rarely forget how you made them feel. Leading by example is a trait of a leader who respects those of authority and the organizational hierarchy. These commanders actively foster collaborative work teams that value others, promote taking responsibility for personal actions, and naturally collaborate well with people.

Mom said not to be a puppet on a string, but once you commit to your employer, adhere to the rules of the organization and give way to authority. Be respectful, follow instructions, and listen to those in charge until they give you a reason to act otherwise. It is wise to heed the advice from those you trust, yet remember your choices are yours to make. Just like Jiminy Cricket tried to advise Pinocchio of the ill fate awaiting him should he join Stromboli's Puppet Show, it was Pinocchio's decision to strike a lifetime contract with Stromboli to become the show's main attraction. It wasn't that Jiminy wanted to pull Pinocchio's strings. His coaching simply fell on wooden ears.

Jiminy was the voice of reason, Pinocchio's mentor, just as Mom was mine. She told me that one day, I would have others who would teach and lead me toward future successes. "Listen to your inner voice and choose your mentor wisely," Fanny warned. "Select one who respects others and treats them with kindness." I appreciated this lesson and am thankful for the dearly departed Jack Williams, my mentor for many years. Jack, like Fanny, helped me find my way. They encouraged, empowered, and inspired me to be my best. Not one time did either of them treat me like a puppet with strings.

THE NOSE THAT GROWS

"LIAR. LIAR. PANTS ON FIRE!" Many of us are familiar with this phrase. It is thought to be a popular idiom dating back to 1945. According to my brother, every time I disagreed with him—and it didn't matter whether he was telling the truth or not—I would snap back with this phrase, which annoyed him but made me feel, well, quite pleased with myself. The rest of the saying includes: "Nose as long as a telephone wire." Often used as a schoolyard taunt, it is less severe when adults say it. However, the undertone of the phrase is evident that when a person lies, he or she may be easily spotted.

For most of the story, things are not looking up for Pinocchio. Instead of being characterized as brave, truthful, and unselfish, Pinocchio makes poor choices and finds himself in the awful predicament of having a nose that grows. For every lie he tells, Pinocchio's nose gets longer. The message within the story subtlety demonstrates the visible consequences of not being truthful. Painful as it was for him, Pinocchio not only tells one lie. He tells three within the same story.

One because he was afraid to lose something he had.

Another to support the first lie.

A third to back up the first two.

Unfortunately, in real life, we do not have the advantage of experiencing the nose-growing of one who chooses to lie to our face. Actually, that would be validating in the moment, but I suspect we'd have many Cyrano de Bergeracs around the world.

As noted in Rule Two, Fanny had no room in a relationship for lying. And she had a clever way of coaching the truth out of you if she thought you were being dishonest. Honesty is a necessary attribute for an effective leader. Ask someone to describe another person's level of integrity, and undoubtedly that description will include words signifying being trustworthy and standing by one's word. An effective leader is by nature a truth seeker, especially if they expect others to follow them. And from the mentee's point of view, it's not just about mimicking the leader's behavior; honesty is something that is deeply rooted in one's integrity.

When we diminish the value of our word, what's left to say? Fanny's Rule: "Make your word mean something, and others will follow your lead." It's always a good practice to say what you mean and mean what you say. She expected me to fill my words with actions that supported what I said I would do. Words without deeds are empty and useless, she would say. Make your words and actions purposeful and inclusive for all.

One can only build excellent and righteous character when the choices of speech and deeds are based on morality and ethical convictions that do not harm others, put the needs of others ahead of your own, and are based on the truth. When we say words that express hate, selfishness, and conceit, the value of what we say and do is diminished. Sometimes to the point of no return.

I believe that we should let our words and actions stand to express the humanness in those that do not think, act, or look like us. For the most part, I suspect Mom's belief in the value of one's word stems from her upbringing during the Great Depression. When material things were hard to come by, a person's word was worth more than what money could buy. It was the commodity of common decency and exchange between people. In one of Fanny's coachings, she asked me to ponder, "If you only had a few words left to say, what would they be and who would hear them?" That teachable moment has stuck with me my entire life, and because of this, I choose my words carefully. It's important to me that someone will remember them when I am gone, that my words brought purpose and meaning to those around me and reflect the honest life I created. Besides, I don't ever want to be caught with my pants on fire, especially my new pair of space pants.

DON'T BE A DONKEY

"STICK TO YOUR GUNS" is characteristically associated with one's refusal to change a personal conviction or action, even after receiving new information. As more and more voices try to alter a person's opinion, telling him or her that their viewpoint is wrong will likely only fuel the stubbornness. Mom was convinced that there was a fine line between being stubborn and showing determination and might.

From a mentee's perspective, remaining resolute might be the act of clinging to a personal belief or conviction, regardless of its origin. Within a mentoring relationship, it is the mentor's responsibility to challenge the mentee to consider various points of view that encourage critical discourse and debate. It is not about trying to convince the mentee to agree with a single line of thinking. It's about exposing fresh ideas and listening to someone else share a different way of thinking. In the mentor role, a vital discernment is uncovering if a person is merely stubborn or standing firm.

Fanny said that the line separating stubbornness from determination is the truth. Opinions are beliefs built from a perception of reality, not necessarily on real and objective facts. When highly opinionated people act in an uncompromising steadfast fashion, they dig in their heels and become closed off to others' views and ideas. This is especially true when a person acts on a selfish accord and makes no attempt to see things from a different or countering advantage point. They remain stuck in their position, not because of their uniqueness, but to make a positional statement of being right. The more PG-rated version of what Fanny said when she saw me being uncompromising and deaf to reason was, "Don't be a donkey." Mom knew the weakness associated with stubbornness drowns out any possible positive outcome.

Fanny coached me to be determined, as described in Rule Seven. She encouraged me to start habits that:

Developed my strength.

Honed my skill.

Learned from the past.

Visualized my successful achievement of a goal or ambition.

In this Rule Eight of finding your Jiminy Cricket, it's about selecting a mentor who will challenge your "status quo." It is to bring about a healthy conversation where respect is earned and agreement is optional.

Stubborn people are difficult for me to understand, mainly because they have generally shut themselves off from the voices of trust and reason. Closing off communication limits the exchange of information and new ideas. It's similar to going from a four-lane highway to a one-way street. This singular approach becomes a roadblock to keep out anyone with a contrary point of view.

No matter how much Jiminy tried to warn Pinocchio of the perils that awaited him on Pleasure Island, the "wooden boy wannabe" stubbornly ventured onward, getting his way. He did this all the while thinking and believing he knew best. The end result for Pinocchio: he became a donkey.

Pinocchio's defiance resulted in harm, not just intrinsically, as it kept him from being a real boy. It affected him physically. Operating consistently in a stubborn state of mind can contribute to poor health. For Pinocchio, his poor health resembled the appearance of a work mule.

The only positive aspect of being stuck in one's ways is that the individual's actions are directed inwardly and not to control others. However, even if the unwavering position may seem moot to others, it does not outweigh the severe consequences of being inflexible and creating unintended harm. Pinocchio's choice to abandon his conscience's wisdom to pursue his own selfish desires directly impacted him and indirectly affected Geppetto.

A mentor's role is to coach the mentee to find the truth. The mentor helps the mentee think differently by exploring new ideas while digging deep below the surface of the concept, transforming stubbornness into determination and expanding one's thoughts to consider multiple points of view. Through the learning process, the two exchange information and challenge the very essence of one's beliefs to find the line of truth.

One afternoon while it was raining, my brother and I were confined to playing inside. We occupied our time and gave our imagination a whirl by creating paper airplanes. With scrap paper in our hands, we built the best aerodynamic version we could. Standing in the hallway behind a broom on the floor—which served as our starting gate—my brother and I would launch our flying creations. The goal was to see who would go the farthest.

Without fail.

I won.

Every time.

My brother became upset and got frustrated because I would not share my secret folds with him. Mom suggested that I teach him how to build a better plane, but I was dead set against that idea. "Why would I want to help him?" kept playing over and over again in my brain. Mom was a little more insistent while I remained steadfast in my position. She continued to encourage me to help him, but that only motivated me to stick to my guns of not helping him. I crossed my arms, tapped my toe, and looked the other way, hoping she would go back to doing the wash and leave us alone. There was no way (in H-E-double-toothpicks) I was going to help him beat me.

After several minutes, Fanny drew the line. She approached me and mimicked my stance. She crossed her arms and tapped her toe. But, instead of looking away, she stared straight into my eyes. It was that dreaded stink eye. Mom sure had a way of getting her point across, and she didn't have to utter a word! Finally, she put her arms around me and whispered, "Don't be a donkey."

Mom had taught that lesson several times before, and even though I wasn't in the mood to budge from my position and help my brother, I knew it was the right thing to do. Fanny used the story of Pinocchio and the donkey to remind me what happens when I act selfishly by closing myself off to helping others. Reluctantly, I gave way to her coaching that day and helped my brother build some aerodynamic planes. All afternoon, we continued to have fun. I still won most of the flights, but he won some, too.

Not every story will have a happy ending, but when it does, we can celebrate it. Pinocchio was eventually transformed from a donkey to a real boy. This change required the help of a Blue Fairy, a Jiminy Cricket, or a mentor. Pinocchio's journey to becoming brave, truthful, and unselfish took many twists and turns. Mainly because he acted on his own accord and downplayed the value of his conscience, Jiminy Cricket.

Today, when young emerging leaders ask me my best advice for becoming successful, I enthusiastically say, "Get a mentor. You will be glad you did." I am more than grateful for those people who served that role in my life.

Transformation of character will not come at the hand of a fairy waving a wand or granting a wish. It will take modeling effective leadership attributes of being teachable, showing compassion, practicing humility, and seeking the truth. From Fanny's perspective, the day I went from being stubborn to mentoring my brother on how to build a better plane was the day I gave up a pair of donkey ears to earn a set of wings.

TEACHABLE MOMENTS

- Puppet on a string—Lead by example, not a string. Leaders want to demonstrate the type of actions they expect from others. Look for mentors and coaches who model behavior built upon integrity. Follow the advice of those who do what they say and mean what they say, given that you align with their moral beliefs and ethical convictions, of course. Effective mentors treat others based upon the Golden Rule of being kind and considerate to others just as one would want others to treat them in return.

- The nose that grows—Honesty is a core value and an essential attribute for effective mentor-mentee relationships. Telling the truth means speaking words based on facts, not opinions. It means being forthcoming and straight-forward without pause or omission of truth. Being honest with others promotes a healthy and trusting relationship built upon candor and transparency.

- Don't be a donkey—Learn the difference between being stubborn and having determination. Avoid being so stuck in a singularly focused mindset. Allow your mentor to challenge your "status quo" thinking to encourage critical discourse and debate.

For your free *Fanny Rules* Teachable Moments Journal go to https://drtroyhall.com/documents/fannyrulesjournal.pdf.

MENTORING LESSONS FOR RULE EIGHT: SELECT YOUR MENTOR

Get a mentor! Listed below are seven steps to finding a mentor and getting started with your mentoring program. Remember, selecting your ideal mentor is much like interviewing for a job, except this time you're asking the questions and doing the hiring.

1. Identify a list of business leaders who are experienced or experts in their fields.
    *   Choose candidates who have at least fifteen years of experience in their chosen field.
    *   Seek referrals for your list from colleagues or others you trust for solid advice.
    *   Be sure to specify what you want in a mentor. For instance, if it is essential that the leader share your faith or beliefs, be clear that it is a requirement.
2. Qualify the candidates on your list by researching their professional profiles on all social media platforms. Ask others about these individuals to determine how they will relate to you and you will potentially learn from them.
3. Narrow down the list to your top two. If you know the number one choice, you can then ask him or her to be your mentor. If not, then you will need to follow some etiquette protocols of engagement. Start with an email, phone call, or face-to-face request, followed by a brief introduction. Have questions prepared to ask your potential mentor and narrow down your selection. Repeat this process until you have made your selection.
4. Set up your mentorship program over a minimum of six months (or longer as needed). It is preferable to schedule

calls every other week at a specified time for thirty to sixty minutes in length. Frequency is up to the two of you, however. Your meetings may require a shorter or longer time in between, depending on homework assignments.

5. Begin your first session with basic introductions, set boundaries for how you will connect, and the liberties you each have for calling or texting during the day or evening. Define what you want to learn from the mentor or choose to work on a specific project. Identify a specific project for you to work on and agree on the homework assignment(s).

6. Each remaining session begins by addressing the previous week's homework assignment. Of course, you may always go off script and customize a meeting or a series of meetings based on what you want to achieve. It is the mentee's responsibility to set the agenda and the appointments. The mentor's role is to provide support and advice.

EXAMPLE OF A MENTORING SESSION ON STUBBORNNESS

Think of a time when you were stubborn about something. Imagine the person you were frustrated with, the circumstances, and how you behaved. Discuss these questions with your mentor.

- How did you feel about your stubbornness?
- What were your "aha" moments once you realized how stubborn you were?
- Discuss the steps you took to move away from being stubborn.
- Identify three steps (at a minimum) you can take that you can do to minimize the times you become positional for no reason.
- Ask yourself who can you turn to for accountability to help you avoid becoming the donkey?

For more information on setting up a Winning Mentoring Program, contact me at drtroyhall@gmail.com.

WHO WILL YOU BE WHEN YOU GROW UP?

"Every oak tree starts as an acorn."

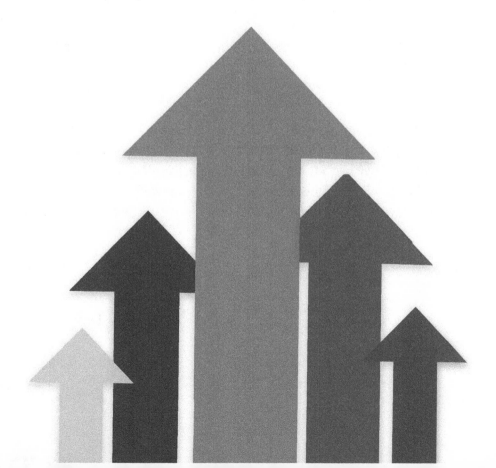

"BE YOURSELF." IT IS NOT ALWAYS EASY.

SOMETIMES IT GETS DOWNRIGHT UGLY and messy to find oneself amid all the emotions and the external push and pulls that can impact choices. Fanny told me that before I present myself to others, I better make sure the "me" is actually what I want others to see. If I want to be a good-hearted person, then I had better act like it, not for show, but for real.

Like the growth of a mighty oak tree, a person's journey of self-discovery begins as an acorn. It's then the individual's responsibility to "grow up," and this responsibility shouldn't be taken lightly. It also takes more than a fairy wish or an apt metaphor. It takes discipline, determination, and a trusted mentor. Fanny's teachable moments were seeds of truth. Mom knew that to help me grow and become the me I was meant to be would require instruction, nurturing, and a little bit of a green thumb.

Water the seed with wisdom.

Nurture it with love and compassion.

Prune and trim the branches that grow awry.

Shape it for a lifetime.

Fanny set out on a journey to teach me these lessons without knowing whether she would survive cancer and having no idea if she would ever see her boy grow into becoming a leader. But she knew she had to try. From bedside to armchair, Fanny offered me many life lessons that taught me to:

1. Learn as much as possible and put that knowledge to use.
2. Treat people well, offering every person respect, dignity, and honesty.
3. Own a positive mind that could achieve anything I wanted to be.
4. Make choices of character, not those bound by circumstance, innuendos, or triviality.

5. Build upon strengths to support growth and development.
6. Think with a creative flair that looks at the inside of the box just as much as outside. Approach problems with innovative solutions that solve needs, not only wants and desires.
7. Acquire discipline in an area of study and exercise determination to keep on track of success.
8. Select a good mentor that challenges a more conservative and traditional way of thinking. Keep open to new possibilities and ideas.
9. Find out who I wanted to be and pursue it with my heart, mind, and soul.

These nine lessons are not just checked box ideas or things to do. Each lesson has its own specific teachable moment, along with strong connections and interdependencies that lead to developing a whole person. Discovering who you want to be is a mentoring journey where you gain knowledge and enlightenment through self-discovery. Arriving at what looks like the destination is often just a resting spot before the next adventure begins. Fanny's Rules authentically came to life and, together with her nuggets of teachable moments, offered wisdom to shape me as a leader.

 ## DON'T CHEAT THE TRUTH

"THE TRUTH IS IN THE 'I AM,' not the 'someday I will be'—don't cheat the truth," Fanny would quip. It took me years to understand what she meant. Mom placed a tremendous value on the "Word" as the truth. She believed the sixty-six books in the Bible, from Genesis to Revelation, were the awe-inspired word of God. Mom's teachings on this topic included the power of the spoken word. She grounded this lesson pointing back to two specific stories in Scripture.

First is the story in Genesis that describes God speaking the world into existence: the power of the spoken word creates the world within which we live. This is why Fanny was so insistent on building a positive mindset. She would say, "If I speak negative words instead of positive ones, it will severely impact how I think of myself. Those negative thoughts would also influence others on how they would see and relate to me in our world."

The second scriptural reference supporting her hypothesis of the "Spoken Word" is contained in the response Moses received to explain who God is to the Israelites. God replied, "I am who I am." Mom told me God did not say, "Someday I will be." God claimed his essence in the present tense of being. Fanny's meaning of "cheating the truth" was that one does not live up to who they have become or who they were meant to be.

When someone affirmatively states who they are, they offer a clear picture of their desired self. It's not as though one is saying he or she has arrived as a perfect self. However, being clear of who one has become then empowers the individual to speak life of who they are into existence and to reinforce it repeatedly. As we know, humans aren't perfect, yet that shouldn't inhibit the growth and development one experiences on the journey.

On the days I did not live up to my best, Mom counseled me to stop portraying a negative image and take positive action. Fanny would remind me, "Say who you want to be out loud and repeat it several times." Mom's instruction let the sound of my voice express meaning and power, always keeping in mind that declaring myself in the present would be seen as purposeful and intentional. She knew this would help "create" me now and for the future, not leaving anything to chance. Fanny also knew people did not want to follow an accidental boss. They'd look to a leader who was self-aware, focused on others' needs, and who treated people fairly and equitably, while creating a trusted environment.

The advice to "be yourself" isn't meant to seem like one has to do a magic trick or express some half-baked approach to "will" this image of yourself into existence. Instead, it is about accessing one's fundamental core values and speaking with confidence, so anyone who heard these values would understand they were real. Fanny did not say, "Be the best job you can be someday." It was, "Be the best person you desire to be in whatever job you are doing."

Claim who you are now.

Own what you claim to be.

Bring your best self to life.

Claiming who you are now is not an example of arrogant pride, but a simple declaration of *your* truth, your very essence of who you are. If you choose to tell everyone how amazing you are, you may want to heed Grandma Goldie's advice and lay off the horn. There is no shame or ridicule when you take ownership of being a loving, kind, gentle, and patient person. Those attributes, along with joy, peace, goodness, faithfulness, and self-control, provide an excellent foundation that translates to being a loyal, reliable, and appreciative partner, a loving parent, an honest person, an innovative entrepreneur, or a creative artist. In fact, when you are totally honest and transparent about who you are, others will see you as approachable, believable, and compassionate.

Every day is an opportunity to move toward the future of being a better version of who you were the day before. This will require putting forth daily effort into shaping your inner values and manifesting them in your beliefs, positive attitudes, and behaviors. It also takes the type of disciplined and determined effort to stay on the path and sometimes sweat integrity bullets to keep from getting distracted in pursuit of the goal at hand.

Early in my career, after receiving a big promotion at work, I was talking with Mom on the phone telling her all about my new title, impressive office with a window—AND a door—along with a nice bump in salary. It was an exciting accomplishment to have achieved the status of manager at a young age. Mom listened intently as I described every detail of how I had finally become what I wanted to be. She expressed her happiness for my newfound success, she congratulated me on my incredible achievement, and she expressed her joy that I had found what I wanted to be. However, knowing Mom as well as I did, her tone indicated that something wasn't right—she hadn't revealed all that was on her mind. I couldn't put my finger on it, but I knew. Without me asking or her telling, we exchanged goodbyes and love yous then ended the call.

The next week, I again thought about the call and wondered what was behind Mom's silence. That following weekend, I called her. On this call, I told her about my colleagues and some of the team-building activities we did that week. Before she even asked me about the ladder, I reassured her, "No one had been stepped on. I earned the promotion on my own merits." I could hear her smile through the phone and her pride that I appeared to have mastered that lesson. We talked some more and laughed at some silly stories my staff shared with me and how I had helped another colleague solve a problem.

As we neared the end of this call, I shared with her that I suspected something more was on her mind at the end of our last call. Mom comforted me and apologized if she had not seemed excited. It was not characteristic of her to be a dream stealer or a joy crusher. She reassured me that she was truly happy for my success, but she did have some concerns last week and wanted to think about them before revealing her thoughts.

In the next few minutes, I understood the difference between the calls. Fanny spoke very clearly: "Last week, I heard a boy talk about achieving what he wanted to be—a job, a title, and some level of status that seemed important. This time, I heard a man speak life to who he is. A leader who takes interest in people, shares life with them, and offers assistance to others when he could simply turn the other way."

It was a classic teachable moment where I more clearly learned how to distinguish the difference between describing what one has achieved in place of who he had become. My success as a manager was not going to be because of the title, the salary, or the office. It was going to be in how I would lead, treat, and respect those reporting to me and how I would be of service to my direct reports and those in other areas of the company. Fanny's biggest concern was in the smallest of details. When one describes success in the what, they give life to the extrinsic factors that come along with the position. A true leader is found within the kindness, compassion, humility, and gentleness of who he or she is. In some simple way, Fanny wanted to make sure I was true to my inner self and projecting it outwardly for others to see, so I would not end up "cheating the truth."

HOLDING THE STONE

"IT ISN'T THE STONE that breaks the house; it's the person throwing it." In other words, an object does not have the power, the person holds the power, and how that person chooses to use the control determines if it is used to empower or oppress. Once again, the mentoring lesson of choice comes back around full circle. One can choose to be a leader or mentor of character and use influential power to build up and affirm others or not. As Fanny would say, "If you speak words of affirmation, you never will be misquoted." Yet some leaders are overtaken by circumstance and wield authoritative power to tear others down. Fanny's advice when she saw this happening: "If you have to tear someone down to build yourself up, you weren't that damn good to begin with."

Here, both of Fanny's lessons illustrate that power can be asserted in either a positive or negative way. In leadership, McClelland's Human Motivation Theory expresses power as one of three central stimuli: affiliation, achievement, and commitment. He describes power as either authoritative or influential, stating that neither power is good nor bad on its own; it is how a person displays the power that determines whether the outcome is empowerment or oppression.

In straightforward terms, leaders use authoritative power to maintain order over chaos. Using power to organize chaos and enforce rules and regulations is not intended to aim harm at a specific demographic profile. Exercising control with the intent to bring order and support standards without inflicting hurt can undoubtedly happen, but far too often, authoritative power is applied to dominate and suppress.

In Fanny's metaphor of the stone and glass house, the person who throws the object is destructive and using authoritative power. They are not breaking the fragile structure to uphold a process requirement or to protect another's dignity. Instead, this power is being used to exert force that inflicts pain with the implied intent to demonstrate the consequences of disobedience.

Only influential power is consistently used for the betterment of the one and the many. Leaders who mold thinking and focus energies on developing positive mindsets use this type of suggestive force to impact or shape how others behave. This power to impact others' actions without applying direct force is a positive, persuasive form of motivation. It allows those affected by its suggestive properties to experience self-discovery. In other words, those impacted by influence can learn from the wisdom of trusted individuals without making the same mistakes on their own.

Effective leaders of transformation utilize both authoritative and influential power to further the desired business outcome or impact a social cause. They know that to be truly transformative, they must put the needs of others first. Neither kind of power on its own is destructive. Again, it's the person wielding power that determines how others feel it.

Is power being used for personal gain?

Does power further a personal agenda or assert a bias?

Can power bring about improved education, cultural enlightenment, and unity?

When I think of power as a destructive force, it reminds me of the story I told in Rule Four about how I let my friend down. As the school kids hurled personal insults at her, they threw the stone to crush her glass house while I stood by silently and did nothing to support her. This made me just as guilty as if I had been holding the stone myself.

Leaders can put power to good use. They can drop the stone and stand up straight and tall. Leaders can be firm in their resolve to:

Exercise positive influence over others and not just authority.

Give people a reason to discard their stones.

Ask them to stand with you and have it mean something.

In her own inevitable fashion, Fanny influenced me to think about who I wanted to be. She taught me the value of setting my actions in motion to reflect that persona. She encouraged and empowered me. Fanny concluded this lesson with a message very similar to that of Alexander Hamilton's philosophy, "If you fail to stand for something, you may never stand for anything." Although, she added… "And you don't need a stone to make your point."

MIRROR—MIRROR

"YOU GET WHAT YOU SEE" may be what one thinks at first blush, but it does not always hold true unless one is exposed from the inside out. Although first impressions are impactful and often essential, it is always best to be as authentic as possible in your interactions with others, whether at home, work, or in social settings. Just as meaningful as it is to not *cheat the truth* of claiming who you want to be here and now, it is equally important to project the real you, exposing your deepest and most guarded values, beliefs, and attitudes. In Fanny speak, "Act positively and be true to yourself. When you do, then others will see and experience the true you."

Recently my niece shared her recollection of another teachable moment between her and Fanny (Grandma "Gma" Frances) as the mentor.

> "After putting crackers in a tin container, I [niece] looked at my reflection on the side of the square can. Using the mirror-like surface to see Gma Frances behind me, I asked her if the cracker's brand mattered. She looked back and smiled. 'It isn't the name on the box that determines the taste, it is the ingredients that go into making the cracker.' Gma Frances suggested I turn over the container and read her the ingredients listed on the label.
>
> Flour.
>
> Water.
>
> Salt.
>
> She brought attention to the simplicity of what was needed to make a good-tasting cracker and how using the right ingredients is relatable to bringing forth one's inner self. Of course, Gma Frances wanted to add honey to make the dry cracker taste sweeter, but she knew that wasn't realistic. But it did give us a good laugh."

Metaphorically speaking, Fanny compared the base ingredients of flour, water, and salt to their core values, beliefs, and attitudes. The flour is like a person's base foundation. Water reflects beliefs, which resembles the ebb and flow (fluidity) between perception and reality. Salt is our attitude or the spice of how we think of life. Mixing these elements and doing the appropriate amount of kneading, cutting, and baking produce a great-tasting cracker.

This process can be said for people, too. When people mix core values, beliefs, and attitudes with attention to the positive, then they are working, cutting, and baking the dough, so a best self emerges. The metaphor of comparing what's inside a cracker to how people build internal values and qualities was a simple lesson yet powerful in meaning. Creating the best version of yourself requires good ingredients. Fanny seemed to have a way to use even the most routine activities to make a point, and often one lesson led to another.

ONE BAD APPLE

MOM WAS CAREFUL to always remind me not to judge people by my first interaction with them. She was of the firm stance that it wouldn't be prudent to make a snap judgment about a person solely based on where they lived, the type of job they had, or how they dressed. She encouraged me to get to know someone and give them a chance. Mom had emphasized this point to my niece during the back-to-school shopping trip mentioned in Rule Four. She made it clear that just because they shopped in a second-hand store did not make them second-handed people.

When we generalize a person's behavior over an entire group, we do injustice to the individuals uncharacteristic of that behavior. Imagine a class of twenty students. Nineteen follow the teacher's instructions. They generally get along with others and promote harmony by following the rules and playing nice with their classmates. But there is this one bad apple in the group who is disruptive, destructive, condescending, and spouts colorful language, words of hatred, and has disgust for anyone not like themselves. What if the teacher then characterized the entire class as if every student is like *them*? Putting a whole group of people under the label of *"them"* minimizes the advancement of unity, equality, and peace. Fanny Rules: "There is a reason unity is part of community."

In this example, it may be clear who is expressing disobedience, selfishness, and dislike, but it should not be applied to everyone in the group. Individual action must be viewed as such, and even though we heard the saying, "One bad apple spoils the whole bunch," it's not the rest of the story. The bad apple only ruins the bunch if those around him or her starts to mimic those values, beliefs, attitudes, and behavior.

This metaphor of associating apples as people in a bunch or group was not about categorizing fruit, situations, or treatment of others. It was about one taking on those behaviors as if they were their own and being guilty by association. The apple, so to speak, was not bad because it was a different variety; it was bad because of the choices it made. In Fanny's teachings, the bad apple example did not mean the entire bunch should be categorized because of one spoiled piece of fruit.

She warned me to be careful who I had as friends, associates, business partners, and trusted advisors. Fanny would tell me that when the bad apple shows up, I have choices to make.

Get out of the way.

Sink in and become one of the bunch.

Stand up and be my own apple.

Unfortunately, I did have an experience when I became one of the bunch and not the good ones, either. This was the story in Rule Four of how I failed to stand up for my friend who was being called names. That lesson taught me to stand up for what I believe in and not let popularity overrule what I know is the priority. I have not made that same mistake twice. I consistently stand up, act fearlessly, take names, and kick some arse along the way.

TEACHABLE MOMENTS

- Don't cheat the truth—claim who you want to be in the present tense: "I am." Start the work-in-progress journey today, not someday, when you think you might be ready to begin. When we're young, we dream of our ideal job when we grow up. Instead of focusing on a title, stature, and the benefits of those things, think about the qualities you want to possess. Once you know who you are, then you can speak life with your words. This will allow you to claim your rightful place of being your best self now and live up to those expectations.

- Holding the stone—understand that the power is not in the object itself; instead it is with the one who uses it. People choose whether to use power to demand action and oppress others or they use it to influence positively and empower others to greatness.

- Mirror, mirror—sometimes to see your inner self, you must first shed who you are to become who you were meant to be. When you look in the mirror and see your reflection, are you the same person on the inside? The mirror does not lie. Allow your inner values to come forth in everything you say and do.

- One bad apple—consider the choices one makes when selecting friendships, business partnerships, and mentorships. Do not judge others because of where they live, the type of job they have, or how they dress. Don't become guilty by association. Take a stand for who you are, not who someone else wants you to be.

For your free *Fanny Rules* Teachable Moments Journal go to https://drtroyhall.com/documents/fannyrulesjournal.pdf.

MENTORING LESSONS FOR RULE NINE: FIND YOURSELF

1. Write down your "I am" statements. Include as many as you'd like. Remember these are your claims for today. You don't have to be perfect to put them down. For instance, you may say something like:
   - I am kind-hearted.
   - I am a person of joy.
   - I am a good leader who thinks of others.

2. For each "I am" statement above, describe the attributes (listed a-g below) that you already have and those you will strive to attain that support your claim.
   - Teachable
   - Compassion
   - Grace
   - Humility
   - Truth-seeking
   - Pure Intentions
   - Peacemaking

3. Discuss with your mentor when you failed to claim your "I am" moment because you were too wrapped up waiting on the *someday*.

4. Consider the consequences suffered when you *cheat the truth* and discuss with your mentor.

5. If you were ever that "bad apple," what was that experience like for you? Who was impacted? How did you resolve any damages or ill feelings of others?

6. What three things do you believe are worth standing up for? Why? For example, I stand up for my friends. Because there are times when relationships need to be protected. I stand up for justice and fair treatment of all. Because I do not believe people should be minimalized or oppressed because they are different from me.

ACTIONS SPEAK LOUDER THAN WORDS

"When you are true to yourself, others can then see the true you."

FINAL THOUGHTS

FANNY WAS AN EXTRAORDINARY WOMAN and the best mentor I ever had. Yet I suspect you have figured that out if you've read this far in the book. She grew up in a small town during some of the most difficult times in our country's tumultuous past. Mom was a brave woman who valiantly fought breast cancer and won. She wasn't a martyr and never asked for a medal. Her body was scarred and ripped to shreds, yet she still had one of the most positive outlooks on life of anyone I have ever known.

When she was diagnosed with breast cancer, Mom made a conscious decision to choose life over circumstance. With what she thought were just months to live, she filled each day with prayers of thankfulness and gratitude. Mom later shared with me that she considered her survival a testament to God and that he had other things for her to do in her lifetime. I believe this is why she lived her life with purpose. I also believe it was her faith that drove her quest to impart all the practical leadership advice she could to me while I sat at her bedside during her recovery.

Known for her shy and quiet demeanor, when Fanny spoke up, people listened. Not because of her eloquent word choices, but for the very essence of the goodness and kindness in her heart. She was always thoughtful, down-to-earth, and meaningful. Her dry sense of humor often broke through the toughest of exteriors. She had a way of allowing people to open up and tell her things they wouldn't even tell their priest.

Mom was wise beyond her years and freely shared her wisdom. She assisted anyone who needed help whether they called upon her or not. Even when times were hard, she shared what we had because she knew in her heart God would always provide. She loved people, even those whose behavior was so darned ugly you'd want to turn away and run. With compassion in her heart, Fanny taught me, "Do not burn your bridges. You just never know when you may need to cross them again."

Building and keeping relationships was important to Mom. She told me it would be better to have one true friend than to know a thousand friendly people. I suspect her desire to build strong relationships with others led her to live by this relational standard, "If you bully your way through life, you are fighting for the wrong reason and with the wrong people."

Mom loved us, especially her Slim, and would stand up to even the biggest of opponents to protect her babies. Some of my happiest moments from childhood were when I was curled up in her lap listening to the beating of her heart. It was a comforting sound, and I felt so safe and secure.

I know it sounds like I am memorializing her, and maybe I am in a way. The truth be told, Fanny was well-liked and admired by many. My friend, Joyce, was quick to let me know these thoughts when she heard I was writing this book about Mom.

"You always knew you were loved by her. Anytime I was at your house, your mom made me feel so comfortable. As you remember, I was a bit on the shy side in my younger years. During our early childhood, she was going to take us to the WBOY-TV studio to be on a local show. I got to your house, and she fed us before we left. It was the first time I ever had cheese on my tuna sandwich.

Troy, I feel that she was as proud of my accomplishments as she was of her own children's. This warmed my soul. Thirty-five years ago, she touched my heart with a special handmade quilt for my baby shower. And yes, I still have the quilt today. The image of opening the gift is so vivid. I am very thankful to have had her in my life and to have been a part of hers."

How happy this makes me to have her legacy live on and influence the lives of those who read this book. Fanny's nine lessons will forever be the rules leaders can use to grow and develop themselves and those they serve.

Today, I live my life like a postcard because Mom instilled in me a positive attitude and the understanding that life is not dictated or influenced by the events that surround me. Remembering Fanny's Rules helps me get back up when I am down and become even more determined to move forward with my aspirations. Without fail, so much of Mom's advice has been passed down to my children, and I know it will not stop there. Her words of wisdom are exactly what people should heed to be the best at what they aspire to be. She was full of life. It seems so unfair that Mom was able to beat cancer and live for forty-three years yet could not fight the effects of dementia that eventually took her life.

So, now in the truest form of Fanny, my dearest mom, I extend the tradition and leave you with one of my rules: "I would rather shoot for the stars and end up on the moon than to never have tried at all."

May this book be more than you could have ever asked for or imagined. Peace now and always.

Dr. Troy

THE WHITE
ROSE

"Who are you?"

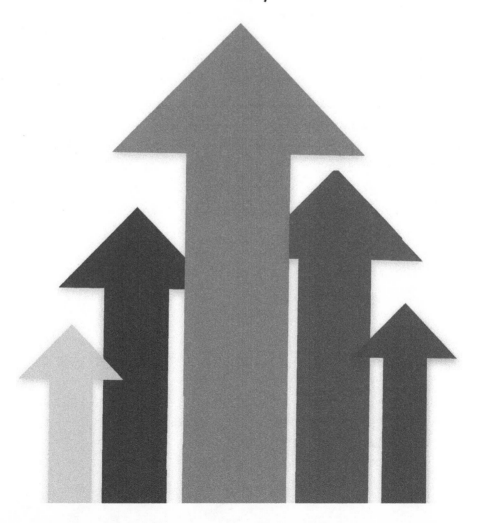

Dearest Caregiver,

As caregivers for a loved one with dementia, there is no joy in being asked those dreadful three words, "Who are you?" You just feel like your total insides have been ripped out and laid upon the ground, exposed for the world to see.

Vulnerable.

Naked.

Uncomfortable.

To make matters worse, you come to the realization that the words were spoken by a person you've known all your life. Someone who has loved you, shared a good time, laughed at you (very deservingly, too, I may add), and seen the "so darn ugly" side of you, it makes you shudder to think you could ever be beautiful again.

After collecting your thoughts, you realize those words weren't said to hurt you. Your loved one said them from an honest place yet a place filled with the terror and fear of not knowing. Something deep down inside tells your loved one they should know who you are, but it isn't coming to the surface.

You will not know for sure but can only imagine it must be like having the answer to a question on the tip of your tongue and yet you can't get it out. It's like being in class, the teacher asks a question on a topic you've studied at nausea, and you cannot for the life of you speak it.

It's there.

Right there.

Just say it.

But the words don't come no matter how much you wished they would.

Vickie and I have had those moments of knowing something and not finding the words to express what we were feeling or thinking. It's scary for us when it happens. We think, "What in the world is wrong with us? Why are our brains not working today?"

Confusion.

Defeated.

Exhausted.

So, if for one moment we can get a grasp of what that feels like to know the answer, to see it right before one's very eyes and yet their brains hide it from them, that is worse than not knowing. Our eyes start to swell, the breathing is accelerated, and the palms begin to sweat. It breaks us...utterly breaks us.

From Troy...during the time Mom lived with us, each evening I would visit her and Dad's apartment we set up in the lower level of our home. When she was lucid, she would smile and give me a nod when I entered the room. Sort of like a debutante would do when one of her men came calling. Those were the times when I thought she just might be getting better.

After making small talk, I would sit down beside her, trying to look into her eyes for reassurance, for love, for recognition. Mom no longer looked at me the same as when I first arrived. Something was different. In an instant, Mom's eyes would go dark. Distant. Hollow. She would so lovingly pick up my hand and look into my eyes with an expression that I can only explain now as a look of doubt and uncertainty. My dearest Fanny would ask, "Who are you?"

I would collect my thoughts.

Look up and smile.

Move in a little closer.

And, in a whisper, "Why, I'm that good-looking man that lives upstairs." Fanny would give me that subtle laugh with a somewhat shy downward turn of her head as if she were playing the role of a perfect southern ingenue at the cotillion. Then looking up at me, Mom would utter with perfect confidence,

"I thought you looked familiar."

One day we will have our white flower, our victory, the first Alzheimer survivor. So, until then, my friends and faithful caregivers, let us march forward into the fields. We must stay vigilant to the end.

Plant the seeds.

Spread the word.

Grow white flowers.

Know that we are the caregivers who spread the hope a cure will be discovered. One day we will rejoice as those loved ones who once were lost to us will now be found.

Until that day, forever and always,

Dr. Troy and Vickie Hall

According to the Alzheimer's Association 2020 Alzheimer's Disease Facts and Figures report, Alzheimer's disease impacts over five million Americans each year. One in three seniors in the United States will pass away with dementia.

These numbers are absolutely staggering. Each and every person impacted is dear to someone, as Mom was to me.

Perhaps there is someone dear to you who is living with Alzheimer's disease. Or perhaps you've already lost someone to the cruelty of Alzheimer's disease or other dementia. I would like you to know that help and hope is out there.

If you are living with or caring for someone with Alzheimer's or other dementia, I urge you to take advantage of the reliable information and support offered through the Alzheimer's Association 24/7 Helpline (800-272-3900). You can also find a wealth of resources and tips at alz.org/help-support.

Finally, if you would like to make a difference in the fight to end Alzheimer's, please visit alz.org to learn about the many ways that you can volunteer, donate, advocate, or participate in meaningful events in your community.

Together, we can change the course of this disease.

BIOGRAPHY

Author | Radio Host | Global Speaker | Talent Retention Strategist and Consultant

Featured on *The Today Show*, ABC, *Beyond the Business Radio Show*, and *CEO World*, Dr. Troy Hall is an award-winning culture strategist, radio show host, speaker, author, and talent retention expert. His doctorate in Global Leadership and Entrepreneurship has sent him across the globe to help leaders create cultures of cohesion and retain top talent in their organizations.

As the author of the best-selling title *Cohesion Culture: Proven Principles to Retain Your Top Talent*, and co-author of a Best New Book Release, *Mission Matters: World's Leading Entrepreneurs Reveal Their Top Tips for Success*, Dr. Troy was once told he did not have the talent to write. His mom, Fanny, reminded him, "It's not the successes or failures that shape your life, it's how you handle them."

With more than forty years of practical leadership experience and a PhD in Global Leadership & Entrepreneurship, Dr. Troy's passion is helping others succeed. His consulting and executive coaching sessions have positively impacted organizational leaders around the globe on how to create cultures of cohesion to retain their top talent.

From the U.S. to Canada and the United Kingdom, from the Middle East to Africa, Asia, Europe, and Australia, Dr. Troy has spoken at global conferences as a subject matter expert on the topics of culture and leadership, strategy, and change.

Currently, Dr. Troy serves as the Chief Strategy Officer for South Carolina Federal Credit Union, and the lead consultant for SCF Solutions, LLC. He is distinguished as an International Development Educator and recipient of the South Carolina State House Resolution for his Global Leadership Exchange program, an international mentoring program.

Dr. Troy developed the industry-recognized mentoring program for the Carolinas Credit Union League Protégé program. Using his executive performance coaching skills, he mentors emerging leaders through the College of Charleston's International MBA program, where he also serves as a consulting advisor.

Dr. Troy has served on the boards of the School of Business for Charleston Southern University and Lowcountry Orphan Relief and is an advocate voice for raising funds and awareness for the South Carolina Chapter of the Alzheimer's Association.

For insights into his award-winning approach of developing a Cohesion Culture™, connect with Dr. Troy. Be sure to take the "Culture Quiz" to determine if your organization is on the right path. And you can connect with him on most social media platforms @ DrTroyHall.

"You don't have to know everything—you just need to be teachable."

—Dr. Troy

ADDITIONAL BOOKS

Cohesion Culture: Proven Principles to Retain Your Top Talent
Best-selling Title (2019) Koehler Books

Mission Matters: World's Leading Entrepreneurs Reveal Their Top Tips for Success
Best New Release (2020) Mr. Century City, LLC

CPSIA information can be obtained
at www.ICGtesting.com
Printed in the USA
BVHW031640110521
607040BV00006B/690